D0633653

The MODERN MULTI-COOKER COOKBOOK

The **MODERN MULTI-COOKER** COOKBOOK

101 recipes for your Instant Pot®

JENNY TSCHIESCHE

Photography by **STEVE PAINTER**

RYLAND PETERS & SMALL

LONDON • NEW YORK

NO LONGER PROPERTY OF
ANYTHINK LIBRARIES/
RANGEVIEW LIBRARY DISTRICT

Senior designer Toni Kay
Editors Gillian Haslam and Miriam Catley
Production manager Gordana Simakovic
Art director Leslie Harrington
Editorial director Julia Charles
Publisher Cindy Richards

Photography & prop styling Steve Painter
Food stylist Lucy McKelvie
Indexer Vanessa Bird

First published in 2018 by
Ryland Peters & Small
20–21 Jockey's Fields
London WC1R 4BW
and 341 E 116th St
New York NY 10029
www.rylandpeters.com

10 9 8 7 6 5 4 3 2 1

Text copyright © Jenny Tschiesche 2018
Design and photographs copyright
© Ryland Peters & Small 2018

Instant Pot® is a registered trademark of Instant Pot Company. It is used here with permission but not associated with this publication. Visit www.instantpot.co.uk or www.instantpot.com for more detailed information on Instant Pot® products and their usage.

ISBN: 978-1-84975-973-1

Printed in China

The author's moral rights have been asserted. All rights reserved. No part of this publication may be reproduced, stored in a retrieval system or transmitted in any form or by any means, electronic, mechanical, photocopying or otherwise, without the prior permission of the publisher.

A CIP record for this book is available from the British Library. US Library of Congress Cataloging-in-Publication Data has been applied for.

Notes:

- Note that the 6-litre/quart Instant Pot® LUX and Instant Pot® DUO models of multi-cooker were used for devising and testing the recipes featured in this book, and preparing them for the photography featured. If you are using an alternative brand of multi-cooker please refer closely to the manufacturer's manual in order to adjust the operating instructions as appropriate for each recipe.
- Both British (Metric) and American (Imperial plus US cups) measurements are included in these recipes for your convenience, however it is important to work with one set of measurements only and not alternate between the two within a recipe.
- All spoon measurements are level unless otherwise specified. A teaspoon is 5 ml, a tablespoon is 15 ml.
- All eggs are medium (UK) or large (US), unless specified as large, in which case US extra-large should be used. Uncooked or partially cooked eggs should not be served to the very old, frail, young children, pregnant women or those with compromised immune systems.

Disclaimer:
The views expressed in this book are those of the author but they are general views only. Ryland Peters & Small hereby exclude all liability to the extent permitted by law for any errors or omissions in this book and for any loss, damage or expense (whether direct or indirect) suffered by a third party relying on any information contained in this book.

Useful Terminology Used in Recipes:

QPR: Quick Pressure Release literally means you manually release the pressure quickly by turning the vent valve on the top of the machine to open. Use a wooden spoon to do this and make sure the vent is not going to expel steam straight onto a socket or any electrical equipment.

NPR: Natural Pressure Release refers to allowing the pot to release built-up pressure naturally. You'll know when it's done because the pressure button will pop back down.

PIP: Pot In Pot means cooking foods in a pot inside your Instant Pot®. This can be used not only to make cakes, omelettes and meatloaves, but also for cooking potatoes or other vegetables at the same time as the meal is cooking.

Inner Pot: This is the stainless steel pot that you do all your cooking in. It's durable and easily washed. I tend to wash, dry and immediately replace the pot so I don't have any mishaps. People have been known to pour water straight into the pot with no inner pot there – that's a quick way to ruin your Instant Pot®.

Deglaze: This is the term used to mean that some liquid will be added and a wooden spoon used to scrape up any tasty bits from the bottom of the pot. This is a necessary step in many recipes to ensure that the dish cooks through and doesn't stop cooking or overheat due to food sticking to the bottom of the pot.

CONTENTS

Introduction **6**
Breakfasts **8**
Soups **20**
Light Bites and Speedy Suppers **38**
Rice and Grains **60**
Curries and Chillies **74**
Casseroles and Roasts **96**
Side Dishes **118**
Sweet Things **128**
Glossary **142**
Index **142**
Acknowledgements **144**

INTRODUCTION

Creating tasty and nutritious meals day after day is what we all aspire to, but it can become a chore. I'm a mum to two children, a health writer, nutritionist, speaker and presenter so, like many people, I'm spinning several plates. How I've wished for a magic gadget that would allow me to throw in a few ingredients and press a button, returning when the time is up to find a delicious meal, ready to eat. A gadget that would be easier and safer to use than an old-fashioned pressure cooker, faster than a slow cooker, yet producing slow-cooked textures and flavours. Reader, such a machine exists and it is called an Instant Pot®. This book will tell you how to use it and get the best from it, and I promise it will change your life (and no, I'm not sponsored by Instant Pot®!).

At its most basic, the Instant Pot® is an electric pressure cooker and slow cooker in one. This description underplays its abilities though, because the Instant Pot® can create the most incredible range of desserts, yogurts, porridge and risottos, too. With this one-pot way of cooking, once supper is in the pot, you can leave it unattended – it's silent, sturdy and very safe. There's a timer on the pot, too, so it can start and stop cooking at specified times, then keep your meal warm until you are ready to eat.

For this book, I've created a collection of recipes that you can recreate yourself without having to master any tricky culinary skills. The book is split into sections based on the type of dish. These are mostly family-size meals with a few exceptions, but even if you are not feeding a family, the bonus is that you can batch-cook meals and save portions in the fridge or freezer (you can even reheat meals from frozen).

The joy of writing this book has been discovering just how easy it is to create delicious and nutritious meals in such a hands-off way. The ingredients I cook with are the kind you will find in your local supermarket. From time to time I might use something from a specialist store, but it's now easy to purchase these ingredients online.

One additional benefit of this method of cooking is that many foods simply taste better – the flavours really shine through. The use of crushed tomatoes in a pasta dish or stew, for example, will make the dish taste sweet and have a great depth of flavour, complementing the vegetables served within the meal. Texturally this way of cooking can also help those who may be a little more particular about certain ingredients. Celery – not always a favourite ingredient – tastes much nicer when pressure cooked, while mushrooms really do absorb flavours. Onions also taste wonderfully sweet once pressure cooked.

Meat and fish textures are much softer using this method of cooking, too. I've worked with many families whose children won't eat meat or fish because they don't like the texture. Most of these children enjoy minced/ground meat so why not beef, lamb, salmon or chicken? A pressure-cooked stew, casserole, chowder or even a whole roast chicken results in meat or fish that simply melts in the mouth.

As far as extra equipment is concerned, I use the trivet that comes with the Instant Pot® to rest fish, vegetables and eggs on, while cooking another element of the whole dish underneath the trivet. I also bought a silicone trivet, a cake 'pan' and steaming basket, as well as a heatproof 1-litre/35-oz. glass Pyrex bowl and a small loaf pan. Scales and measuring jugs/cups are handy, particularly for getting ratios of pasta or rice to water correct. This is one area where it pays to be precise, otherwise you'll end up with a sloppy meal with too much liquid or a burnt meal that simply won't cook because the Instant Pot® will overheat.

If you are new to this way of cooking, I recommend you start by following the recipes, then once you've got your confidence, you can experiment with your own flavours and preferences. The recipe methods use abbreviations and these are explained on page 4, so refer back to them as necessary.

BREAKFASTS

GRAIN-FREE BIRCHER MUESLI

20 g/2 tablespoons ground flaxseeds/linseeds
25 g/3 tablespoons pumpkin seeds
25 g/2½ tablespoons chia seeds
60 g/½ cup sunflower seeds
40 g/scant ½ cup ground almonds
2 eating apples, cored and grated
1 teaspoon ground cinnamon
¼ teaspoon ground ginger
200 ml/¾ cup coconut milk
200 g/¾ cup apple purée (see page 12)

TO SERVE
Greek yogurt
yacon or maple syrup

Serves 3

A great way to enjoy a filling grain-free porridge alternative for breakfast.

Place all the ingredients in a 1-litre/35-oz heatproof glass bowl and stir well.

Place 250 ml/1 cup water in the multi-cooker. Place the trivet in the inner pot. Pop the glass bowl on top.

Secure the lid in place and set to Manual or High Pressure for 3 minutes. At the end of cooking, use the QPR method (see page 4).

Serve each portion topped with a spoonful of yogurt and a drizzle of yacon or maple syrup.

SIMPLE DAIRY-FREE, GLUTEN-FREE PORRIDGE

70 g/¾ cup gluten-free porridge/rolled oats (or 35 g/¼ cup oats and 35 g/¼ cup buckwheat or quinoa flakes)
250 ml/1 cup rice, almond or coconut milk

Serves 2

This simple porridge is fairly flexible in terms of the grains used. I tend to combine protein-rich buckwheat or quinoa with oats as both have quite a strong flavour by comparison to oats. You could, however, make the porridge with just buckwheat or just quinoa flakes if you wished.

Put the porridge/rolled oats and buckwheat or quinoa flakes, if using, and milk in a heatproof glass bowl and stir.

Place 500 ml/2 cups water in the multi-cooker and add the trivet. Place the glass bowl on top.

Secure the lid in place and set to Manual or High Pressure for 10 minutes. At the end of cooking, use the QPR method (see page 4).

Note: you can double this recipe to serve 4 people.

APPLE PURÉE

8 large eating apples, peeled, cored and cut into wedges
70 ml/5 tablespoons apple juice
¾ teaspoon ground cinnamon
¼ teaspoon ground cloves

Serves 6

Apple purée is great in the bircher recipe on page 11. It also makes a quick and tasty dessert when served with yogurt and sprinkled with cinnamon.

Put all the ingredients into the multi-cooker. Secure the lid in place and set to Manual or High Pressure for 6 minutes. At the end of cooking, use the QPR method (see page 4).

Pop the mixture into the bowl of a food processor or use a stick blender to blend to a smooth purée.

RHUBARB AND RASPBERRY COMPOTE

5 sticks of rhubarb, chopped into 3-cm/1¼-in. pieces
400 g/4 cups raspberries
⅛ teaspoon stevia powder

TO SERVE
Greek yogurt

Serves 8

A wonderfully red and deliciously fruity compote to serve over Greek yogurt.

Put 200 ml/¾ cup water into the base of the multi-cooker and add the trivet. Place the fruit in a 1-litre/35-oz heatproof glass bowl and sprinkle over the stevia. Cover the bowl with foil and place on top of the trivet.

Secure the lid in place and set to Manual or High Pressure for 20 minutes. At the end of cooking, use the QPR method (see page 4).

Remove the foil and once the compote has cooled a little, place it in the bowl of a food processor and process to a slightly chunky compote texture. Serve over Greek yogurt.

RASPBERRY CRISP

335 g/3¼ cups fresh or frozen raspberries (defrosted if frozen)
⅛ teaspoon stevia powder
60 g/½ cup chopped roasted hazelnuts
60 g/⅔ cup ground almonds
40 g/½ cup quinoa flakes
50 g/3 tablespoons ghee
2 teaspoons date syrup or honey

Serves 4–6

Based on the more traditional apple crisp, here I've used juicy raspberries and a crunchy topping made of nuts and quinoa flakes.

Place the raspberries in a 1-litre/35-oz heatproof glass bowl. Sprinkle over the stevia and mash the raspberries down with the back of a fork.

In a separate bowl, mix the chopped hazelnuts, almonds, quinoa flakes, ghee and date syrup or honey. Spoon this mixture over the raspberries. Cover the bowl with foil.

Place 200 ml/¾ cup water in the inner pot of the multi-cooker. Put the trivet inside the pot, then the glass dish on top.

Secure the lid in place, then set to Manual or High Pressure for 10 minutes. At the end of cooking, use the NPR method (see page 4).

Enjoy as is or with Greek yogurt or coconut milk yogurt.

SPELT BANANA BREAD

140 g/1 1/4 sticks soft butter
95 g/1/2 cup coconut sugar
2 eggs
2 bananas, mashed
135 g/1 cup wholemeal/ whole-wheat spelt flour
2 1/2 teaspoons baking powder

a 15-cm/6-inch circular springform cake pan or a 15 x 8 x 5-cm/6 x 3 1/4 x 2-inch non-stick mini loaf pan

Makes 1 loaf

A deliciously moist banana bread made with spelt flour.

In a bowl, mix together the butter and sugar. Add the eggs and mashed banana and stir. In a separate bowl, mix the flour and baking powder. Add the dry mixture to the wet mixture and combine. Pour into the cake or loaf pan.

Place the cake or loaf pan on the trivet. Add 450 ml/scant 2 cups water to the multi-cooker, then lower the trivet and cake or loaf pan into the inner pot.

Secure the lid in place and set to Manual or High Pressure for 30 minutes. At the end of cooking, use the NPR method (see page 4) for 15 minutes, then use QPR. Be careful when you remove the lid not to drip any liquid onto the loaf. If necessary, dab off water using paper towels.

Allow the loaf to cool a little before removing from the pan and leaving on a wire rack to cool completely. Serve in thick slices.

GRAIN-FREE BREAD

50 g/1/2 cup macadamia nuts
20 g/2 tablespoons ground flaxseeds/linseeds
15 g/1 3/4 tablespoons coconut flour
1/2 teaspoon bicarbonate of/baking soda
1/4 teaspoon salt
20 g/4 teaspoons ghee, coconut oil or butter
1 1/2 teaspoons honey or maple syrup
1/2 teaspoon apple cider vinegar
3 eggs

a 15 x 8 x 5-cm/6 x 3 1/4 x 2-inch non-stick mini loaf pan

Makes 1 loaf

This is a delicious and nutritious fibre-rich loaf made without grains. As well as being a great breakfast bread, it is delicious served with the chicken liver pâté recipe on page 41.

In a food processor, grind the nuts, flaxseeds/linseeds, coconut flour, bicarbonate of/baking soda and salt. Add the ghee, oil or butter, the honey or syrup, vinegar and eggs. Process again to a batter. Pour the mixture into a mini loaf pan.

Place the loaf pan on the trivet. Add 450 ml/scant 2 cups water to the multi-cooker, then lower the trivet and loaf pan into the inner pot.

Secure the lid in place and set to Manual or High Pressure for 30 minutes. At the end of cooking, use the QPR method (see page 4).

Allow the loaf to cool a little, then remove from the loaf pan and leave on a wire rack to cool completely.

SOUPS

CARROT AND GINGER SOUP

1 tablespoon olive oil or butter
2 onions, diced
1 celery stalk, sliced into 2-cm/3/4-in. pieces
1 tablespoon crushed garlic
1 tablespoon freshly grated ginger
1 1/2 teaspoons ground cumin
1/2 teaspoon ground coriander
1 1/2 teaspoons salt
3 medium tomatoes, cut into quarters
500 g/1 lb. 2 oz. carrots, peeled and sliced into 2-cm/3/4-in. pieces
150 ml/2/3 cup coconut milk

Serves 4

This is a simple soup that is packed full of flavour. The tomatoes in the recipe give a layer of tangy sweetness to the soup.

Press the Sauté button on the multi-cooker. Add the oil or butter to the pot. When hot or melted, add the onions and celery and stir. Cook for 3–4 minutes, then add the garlic, ginger, cumin, coriander and salt and stir to combine.

Add the tomatoes and carrots and stir again to deglaze the pan (see page 4). Add the coconut milk and 250 ml/1 cup water and stir.

Secure the lid in place and set to Manual or High Pressure for 6 minutes. At the end of cooking, use the NPR method (see page 4) for 7 minutes, then use QPR. Use a stick blender or food processor to process the soup to your desired consistency, then reheat and serve.

CURRIED CHICKPEA SOUP

45 ml/3 tablespoons olive oil
15 g/1/3 cup freshly chopped coriander/cilantro
2 onions, finely chopped
2 garlic cloves, finely chopped
1 teaspoon finely chopped fresh ginger
10 cherry tomatoes
2 tablespoons tomato paste
1/2 teaspoon ground cinnamon
1 teaspoon ground cumin
1/2 teaspoon ground coriander
1 teaspoon ground turmeric
220 g/1 1/3 cups dried chickpeas, soaked overnight in water, drained and rinsed the next day
1 vegetable stock cube or 1 tablespoon vegetable stock paste (see page 31)

Serves 4

Using dried legumes and pulses is a really cost-effective way of producing nourishing family meals. Here dried chickpeas require overnight soaking in water.

Press the Sauté button on the multi-cooker. Add the olive oil to the pot. When hot, add the coriander/cilantro, onions, garlic and ginger and sauté, stirring constantly, for about 3–4 minutes.

Add the cherry tomatoes and tomato paste. Stir again for about 2 minutes to deglaze the pan (see page 4), then add the cinnamon, cumin, coriander and turmeric. As soon as these are absorbed into the dish, add the chickpeas, stock cube or vegetable stock paste and 500 ml/2 cups water.

Secure the lid in place and set to Manual or High Pressure for 20 minutes. At the end of cooking, use the NPR method (see page 4) to let the flavours mellow. Good served with natural yogurt and a sprinkling of chopped red onion over the top.

CAULIFLOWER, WHITE SWEET POTATO AND CHORIZO SOUP

1 tablespoon olive oil
2 onions, halved and sliced
100 g/3½ oz. chorizo, chopped into bite-sized pieces
1 large cauliflower, chopped into very large pieces
650 g/1 lb. 7 oz. white sweet potatoes, peeled and chopped into 3 x 3-cm/1¼ x 1¼-in. cubes
200 g/7 oz. passata/strained tomatoes
1 tablespoon salt
1 tablespoon pomegranate molasses or 3 tablespoons grated cheese, to garnish

Serves 6

This is a mellow combination of satisfying salty and sweet flavours. White sweet potatoes are increasingly available in Asian stores and supermarkets, but if you cannot find them simply use orange sweet potatoes.

Press the Sauté button on the multi-cooker. Add the oil to the pot. When hot, add the onions and chorizo and cook, stirring, for 4 minutes. Add all the other ingredients except the molasses or cheese, plus 750 ml/3 cups water.

Secure the lid in place and set to Manual or High Pressure for 5 minutes. At the end of cooking, use the NPR method (see page 4) for at least 20 minutes or until the valve pops back down.

Serve in deep bowls with a drizzle of pomegranate molasses over the top. Alternatively, top with some grated cheese.

CAULIFLOWER AND BACON SOUP

1 tablespoon ghee or butter
2 onions, chopped
5 slices of streaky bacon, chopped
1 large cauliflower, chopped into large florets
1 tablespoon vegetable stock paste (see page 31) or 1 vegetable stock cube
1 teaspoon tamari or coconut aminos

Serves 4

A classic combination – cauliflower and bacon are just made for each other.

Press the Sauté button on the multi-cooker. Add the ghee or butter to the pot. When melted, add the onions and bacon. Cook for about 4 minutes, stirring regularly, then add the cauliflower, stock paste or cube, tamari or coconut aminos and 800 ml/3⅓ cups water.

Secure the lid in place and set to Manual or High Pressure for 6 minutes. At the end of cooking, use the QPR method (see page 4), then process using a stick blender or a food processor, reheat and serve.

BUTTERNUT SQUASH, SPINACH AND CHICKPEA SOUP

1 tablespoon ghee or coconut oil
1 onion, halved and sliced
350 g/12 oz. butternut squash (peeled weight), chopped into 2 x 2-cm/¾ x ¾-in. cubes
3 tablespoons mild korma paste
½ teaspoon salt
freshly squeezed juice of ½ small lemon
1 x 400-g/14-oz. can chickpeas, drained and rinsed (240 g/ 8½ oz. drained weight)
1 x 400-ml/14-fl. oz. can coconut milk
175 g/6 oz. frozen spinach
300 ml/1¼ cups vegetable stock, made with 1 teaspoon vegetable stock paste (see page 31), or ½ vegetable stock cube and 300 ml/1¼ cups water

Serves 4

This is a very satisfying soup with a mild yet warming curry flavour.

Press the Sauté button on the multi-cooker. Add the ghee or coconut oil to the pot. When hot, add the onion and stir until translucent. Add the butternut squash and stir. Then stir in the korma paste, salt, lemon juice, chickpeas, coconut milk, spinach and stock, being sure to deglaze the pot at this stage (see page 4).

Secure the lid in place and set to Manual or High Pressure for 15 minutes. At the end of cooking, use the QPR method (see page 4).

CHICKPEA, POTATO AND BACON SOUP

1 tablespoon butter
1 onion, thinly sliced
130 g/5 oz. chopped bacon or lardons
2 carrots, sliced into discs
1 courgette/zucchini, thickly sliced into discs
350 g/12 oz. potatoes, peeled and cubed
1 x 400-g/14-oz. can chickpeas, drained and rinsed
500 ml/2 cups beef stock or broth (if not salted, add extra salt to taste)

Serves 4

The chickpeas and potatoes give this soup a creaminess that makes it taste more luxurious than its basic ingredients might suggest.

Press Sauté on the multi-cooker. Add the butter to the pot. When melted, add the onion, bacon, carrots and courgette/zucchini. Stir for about 5 minutes until the onion is almost transparent. Add the potatoes, chickpeas and beef stock and deglaze the pot (see page 4).

Secure the lid in place and set to Manual or High Pressure for 4 minutes. At the end of cooking, use the QPR method (see page 4). Serve in bowls with slices of buttered toasted sourdough or grain-free bread (see page 19).

SAM'S SOUP

1 tablespoon ghee or butter
1 onion, chopped
3 carrots, chopped
75-g/2½-oz. pack diced pancetta
1½ stock cubes or 1½ tablespoons vegetable stock paste (see page 31)
400 g/14 oz. (drained weight) canned chickpeas (which means more than one can will be required)

Serves 4

A recipe created by my ravenous son on a whim one afternoon. Now, of course, it is his favourite soup and none of my soups are as good as his!

Press the Sauté button on the multi-cooker. Add the ghee or butter to the pot. When melted, add the onion, carrots and pancetta. Stir for about 5 minutes until the onion is almost translucent. Add the stock cube or vegetable stock paste and a little water to deglaze the pot (see page 4). Then add 750 ml/3¼ cups water and the chickpeas.

Secure the lid in place and set to Manual or High Pressure for 2 minutes. At the end of cooking, use the QPR method (see page 4). Use a stick blender or food processer to blend to your desired consistency, then reheat and serve.

FRENCH ONION SOUP

2 tablespoons butter
1 teaspoon olive oil
4 onions, halved and sliced
135 ml/⅔ cup white wine
3 garlic cloves
2 sprigs of fresh thyme
2 tablespoons vegetable stock paste (see below) or 2 vegetable stock cubes

TO SERVE
Worcestershire sauce (gluten-free, if you wish), grated Parmesan or pecorino and fresh thyme leaves

Serves 4

The ingredients for this classic soup are cost-effective, but the depth of flavour comes from cooking the onions for as long as it takes for them to become brown and sweet.

Press the Sauté button on the multi-cooker. Add the butter and oil to the pot. When the butter has melted, add the onions and stir regularly until they are soft and browning. If they start to stick to the base of the pot, use a little wine to deglaze (see page 4). Add more wine and the garlic and stir until the wine is almost evaporated. Add the thyme, stock paste or cubes and 1 litre/1 quart water and stir.

Secure the lid in place and set to Manual or High Pressure for 7 minutes. At the end of cooking, use the NPR method (see page 4). Add a little Worcestershire Sauce and grated cheese before serving, and scatter over some fresh thyme leaves.

VEGETABLE STOCK PASTE

160 g/5½ oz. vegan cheese or pecorino, grated
3 garlic cloves, finely chopped
200 g/7 oz. celery heart, very finely chopped
3 tomatoes, very finely chopped
130 g/4½ oz. mushrooms, very finely chopped
2 large leeks, finely chopped
2 carrots, finely chopped
1 large onion, finely chopped
2 tenderstem broccoli/broccolini, chopped
1 teaspoon ground turmeric
1 tablespoon dried oregano
1 tablespoon freshly chopped parsley
55 ml/3½ tablespoons apple cider vinegar
2 tablespoons olive oil
100 g/½ cups salt

Makes 2.5 x 500 ml/18 fl. oz. jars

This is used in many of the recipes in this book as I prefer to use stock paste to cubes as I know what's gone into homemade paste. In all the recipes where stock paste or cube is called for, you can use 1 stock cube or 1 tablespoon stock paste interchangeably. Thanks to my friend and Instant Pot® expert Maria for the basis of this recipe.

The quickest way to prepare this stock is to blitz the cheese, garlic and vegetables in a food processor to reduce the amount of fine chopping required. Once you have the base, simply put this in the multi-cooker, along with all the remaining ingredients, secure the lid in place, then set to Manual or High Pressure for 10 minutes. At the end of cooking, use the QPR method (see page 4).

When cool, blitz again in the food processor to a paste. Place in sterilized glass jars and seal the lids, then store in the fridge for up to 6 weeks or in the freezer (leave room for expansion in the jars if freezing).

DAIRY-FREE FISH CHOWDER

2 shallots, sliced using a mandolin on level 1
½ large bulb of fennel, sliced using a mandolin on level 1
1 medium sweet potato, peeled and diced
10 mushrooms, quartered
1 tablespoon freshly chopped flat-leaf parsley
½ teaspoon salt
400-ml/14-fl. oz. can coconut milk
300-g/10½-oz. pack fish pie mix

Serves 2–3

The soup is cooked first and the bite-sized pieces of fish added afterwards to ensure both are cooked perfectly and come together in harmony at the end.

Put the shallots, fennel, sweet potato, mushrooms, parsley, salt and about 220 ml/1 cup coconut milk into the multi-cooker. Secure the lid in place and set to Manual or High Pressure for 3 minutes. At the end of cooking, use the QPR method (see page 4), then open the lid.

Press the Sauté button and add the fish plus the remaining coconut milk. Heat for about 3–4 minutes until the fish is just cooked through (it should start to flake apart). Serve immediately.

BONE BROTH

500 g/1 lb. 2 oz. chicken, turkey, beef or lamb bones, ideally organic
3 carrots
3 celery stalks
1 onion
a couple of bay leaves
some black peppercorns
1 tablespoon apple cider vinegar
3 drops of fish sauce

Serves 4

Bone broths provide protein and minerals. These can support the body's natural detoxification process, improve iron levels and aid digestive health, too. Use a chicken carcase, or buy some bones from your local butcher (you can use turkey, beef or lamb bones, too). Ideally choose organic bones. You need at least 500 g/1 lb. 2 oz.

Put the bones into the multi-cooker, then add in all the other ingredients. Add water to the pot, roughly up to the 4-litre/1 gallon mark.

Secure the lid in place and set to Manual or High Pressure for 120 minutes. At the end of cooking, use the NPR method (see page 4).

Strain the broth using a colander. Store the broth in sterilized glass jars or in a glass bowl in the fridge. A layer of fat will rise to the surface – skim this off once it hardens. The broth can also be frozen for future use (leave a little room for expansion in the jars if freezing).

CHESTNUT AND VEGETABLE SOUP

1 tablespoon olive oil
1 onion, chopped
2 celery stalks, sliced
1 large carrot, chopped
1 courgette/zucchini, chopped
250 g/9 oz. chestnut purée
150 g/2 cups chopped mushrooms
750 ml/3¼ cups vegetable stock or 2 tablespoons vegetable stock paste (see page 31) plus 750 ml/3¼ cups water
freshly chopped flat-leaf parsley
salt and freshly ground black pepper

Serves 4

Nothing says 'autumn' more than this soup! This is the perfect comforting soup to return home to after a walk in the countryside.

Press the Sauté button on the multi-cooker. Add the oil to the pot. Allow it to heat a little, then add the onion, celery, carrot and courgette/zucchini. Stir for about 5 minutes. Add the chestnut purée, mushrooms and stock and deglaze the pan (see page 4).

Secure the lid in place and set to Manual or High Pressure for 4 minutes. At the end of cooking, use the QPR method (see page 4). Allow to cool a little, then use a food processor or stick blender to blend to your desired consistency, then reheat. Season to taste.

Serve in bowls with slices of buttered toasted sourdough or Grain-free Bread (see page 19).

SPLIT PEA AND BACON SOUP

1 tablespoon olive oil
1 large onion, chopped
2 celery stalks, finely chopped
2 carrots, finely chopped
4 slices of streaky bacon, chopped into small pieces
½ teaspoon ground cumin
1 vegetable stock cube or 1 teaspoon vegetable stock paste (see page 31)
340 g/1¾ cups split green peas, well rinsed

Serves 4–6

This is such a comforting soup and a great way of using up the vegetables left in the fridge at the end of the week.

Press the Sauté button on the multi-cooker. Add the oil to the pot. When hot, add the vegetables and bacon. Stir for about 5 minutes until the onion is just becoming translucent. Add the cumin and stock cube or paste and stir well. Add the split peas and 1 litre/1 quart water and deglaze the pot (see page 4).

Secure the lid in place and set to Manual or High Pressure for 10 minutes. At the end of cooking, use the NPR method (see page 4) and serve warm.

VEGETABLE AND BACON SOUP

1 tablespoon olive oil, avocado oil, butter or ghee
2 large leeks, sliced and washed thoroughly
2 carrots, peeled and diced
130 g/1 cup chopped bacon or lardons
2 potatoes (each about the size of a medium jacket potato), peeled and diced
generous ½ teaspoon salt
½ teaspoon dried thyme
1 bay leaf
200 g/2 cups grated/shredded cheese
freshly cracked black pepper

Serves 4

This is one of those meals you'll be thankful for after a hard day when you really cannot be bothered to make a whole meal. It's a very simple but flavoursome soup.

Press the Sauté button on the multi-cooker. Add the oil, butter or ghee to the pot. Leave for a couple of minutes to heat or melt, then add the leeks, carrots and bacon. Stir for about 8–10 minutes until the leeks are soft. Add the potatoes, salt, thyme, bay leaf and 500 ml/2 cups water and deglaze the pot (see page 4).

Secure the lid in place and set to Manual or High Pressure for 6 minutes. At the end of cooking, use the QPR method (see page 4). Serve in bowls with the grated/shredded cheese and some freshly cracked black pepper over the top.

LIGHT BITES AND SPEEDY SUPPERS

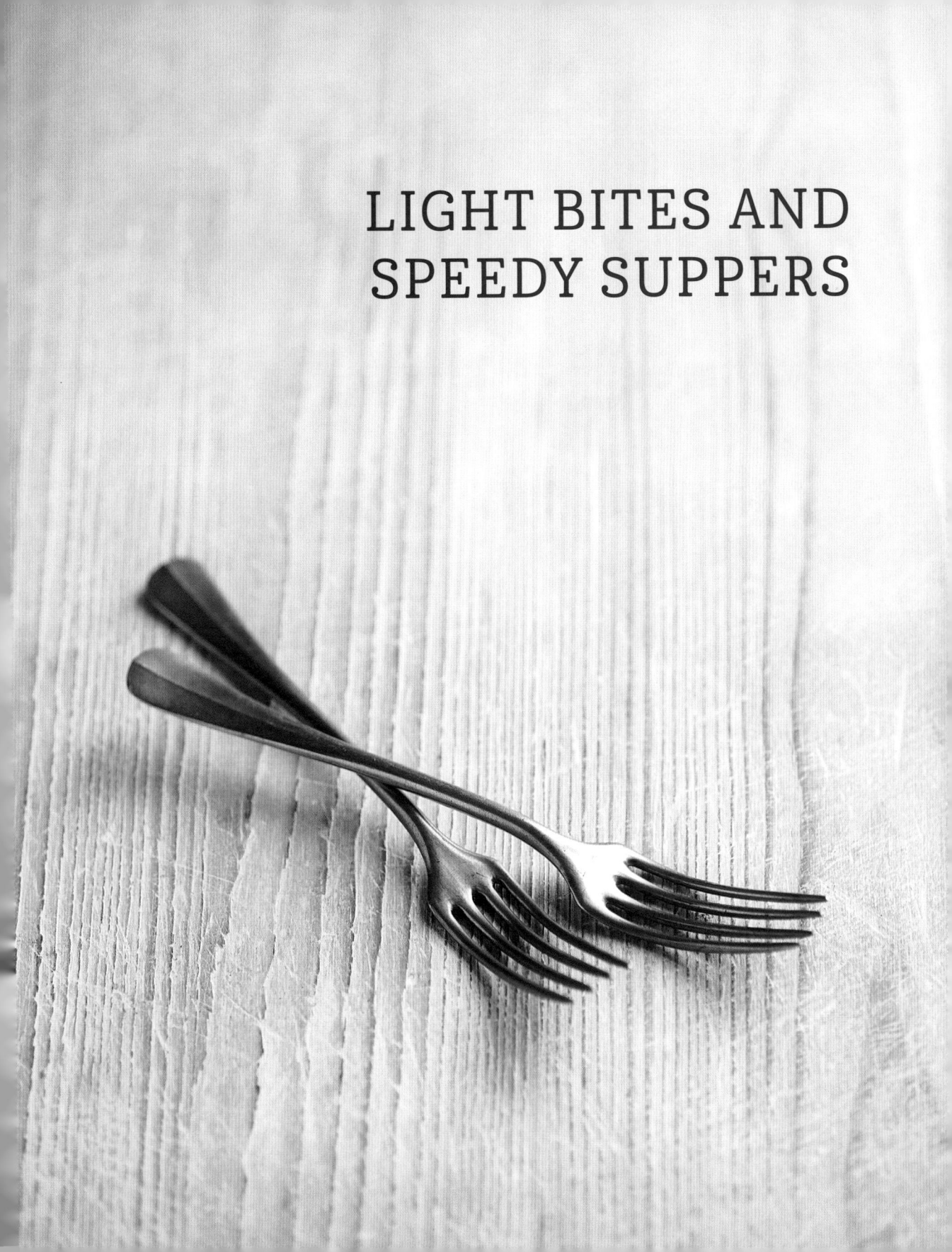

CARROT AND CASHEW HUMMUS

4 medium carrots (about 200 g/7 oz. in total)
1 x 400-g/14-oz. can chickpeas, drained and rinsed
2 tablespoons extra virgin olive oil
1 tablespoon cashew butter
1 teaspoon raw honey
1 teaspoon water
1 teaspoon ground cumin
½ garlic clove, peeled
salt and freshly ground black pepper

Serves 6

This fragrant hummus is a hit with younger palates due to its warming spices and naturally sweet flavour. It's delicious served with fresh vegetable crudités.

Place 250 ml/1 cup water in the base of the multi-cooker, then add the trivet to the inner pot. Peel, top and tail the carrots and place on the trivet.

Secure the lid in place and set to Manual or High Pressure for 7 minutes. At the end of cooking, use the QPR method (see page 4).

Transfer the carrots to a food processor. Add all the remaining ingredients and process to a hummus consistency. Season to taste.

CHICKEN LIVER PÂTÉ

2 tablespoons butter or ghee
1 onion, chopped
75 g/2½ oz. cubed pancetta
400 g/14 oz. chicken livers, trimmed
200 g/7 oz. mushrooms, cut into quarters
1 tablespoon tamari or coconut aminos
2 tablespoons red wine
salt and freshly ground black pepper

Serves 10

Chicken liver pâté is probably the 'safest' way to introduce those who are wary of offal to something new and tasty. It's a cost-effective, nutrient-rich dish and can be served just cooled with a salad or chopped vegetables.

Press the Sauté button on the multi-cooker and add the butter or ghee to the pot. When melted, add the onion. Stir until soft, then add the pancetta and livers. Brown the livers a little, then add the mushrooms, tamari or coconut aminos and red wine, ensuring you deglaze the pan at this stage (see page 4).

Secure the lid in place and set to Manual or High Pressure for 0 minutes. At the end of cooking, use the NPR method (see page 4).

Transfer the mixture to a food processor and process to a very smooth consistency. Season to taste and process again. Leave to cool a little, then enjoy. It will keep in an airtight container in the fridge for 3 days.

SWEET POTATO AND PANCETTA FRITTATA

100 g/3½ oz. diced pancetta
1 medium sweet potato, peeled
1 small onion
8 eggs
½ teaspoon dried mixed herbs
¼ teaspoon garlic powder
¼ teaspoon salt

a 20-cm/8-in. round silicone cake pan

Serves 2

This exceptionally tasty savoury slice makes for a delicious brunch, but once cooled it is fantastically portable for packed lunches or as part of a picnic.

Press the Sauté button on the multi-cooker. Add the pancetta to the pot and sauté until cooked. Remove from the pot and place in the base of the silicone cake pan.

Finely chop the sweet potato and onion in a food processor. Add the eggs, herbs, garlic powder and salt to the food processor and process again. Pour this mixture over the top of the cooked pancetta in the cake pan. Pour 250 ml/1 cup water into the multi-cooker and deglaze the pan (see page 4). Place the cake pan on the trivet and lower into the multi-cooker.

Secure the lid in place and set to Manual or High Pressure for 30 minutes. At the end of cooking, use the QPR method (see page 4). You may need to dab away any excess liquid on the frittata using paper towels.

The frittata can be sliced and served warm or cold. It will keep in an airtight container in the fridge for 3 days.

SPINACH AND SALMON EGG CUPS

¼ teaspoon olive oil
4 large eggs, beaten in a bowl
2 blocks of frozen spinach, defrosted (about 60 g/2 oz. frozen weight in total)
100 g/3½ oz. smoked salmon, thinly sliced or shredded
salt and freshly ground black pepper

4 ramekins

Serves 4

These little ramekins of creamy egg and salty salmon with delicious and nutritious spinach are a real treat.

Using a pastry brush, brush the insides of the four ramekins evenly with the oil.

To the bowl of beaten eggs, add the defrosted spinach and salmon, then season with salt and pepper. Pour the mixture evenly into the greased ramekins. Place 250 ml/1 cup water in the base of the inner pot. Add the trivet on top and place the ramekins on top of the trivet.

Secure the lid in place and set to Manual or High Pressure for 6 minutes. At the end of cooking, use the QPR method (see page 4) and serve immediately. The eggs may have risen during cooking, but they'll soon retract back into the ramekins.

SALMON SUPPER WITH SWEET POTATOES

2 medium sweet potatoes, peeled and cubed
2 salmon fillets
1 x 200-g/7-oz. pack mixed vegetables for steaming (such as French/green beans, tenderstem broccoli/broccolini and asparagus)
1 teaspoon olive oil
salt and freshly ground black pepper
1 tablespoon butter

Serves 2

Salmon is such a popular fish and is so easy to cook in a multi-cooker. This meal for two is a very straightforward dish that will surprise you with its simplicity and speed to plate.

Place 250 ml/1 cup water in the multi-cooker. Put the sweet potato cubes into the water. Add the trivet and place the fish and mixed vegetables on the trivet. Drizzle the oil over the fish and vegetables and season with salt and pepper.

Secure the lid in place and set to Manual or High Pressure for 2 minutes. At the end of cooking, use the QPR method (see page 4). Remove the trivet, drain the sweet potatoes and serve the fish and vegetables with the sweet potatoes and the butter shared between the two plates.

SMOKED SALMON KEDGEREE

Whilst traditional kedgeree is made with smoked haddock and without added vegetables, I've switched things up a little by adding in beans and spinach and serving with smoked salmon. It's a very tasty alternative to the traditional version.

1 tablespoon ghee
1 onion, chopped
approx. 20 French/green beans, topped, tailed and chopped into 1-cm/½-in. lengths
2 garlic cloves, crushed
1 green chilli/chile, finely chopped
1 teaspoon ground turmeric
¾ teaspoon ground cumin
1 teaspoon smoked paprika
1 teaspoon nigella/black onion seeds
¾ teaspoon salt
250 g/1½ cups basmati rice
4 blocks of frozen spinach (about 120 g/4 oz. frozen weight in total)
300–400 g/10½–14 oz. smoked salmon, cut into strips (or buy smoked salmon 'scraps' from your fishmonger)
4 eggs, hard-boiled/cooked, shelled and quartered

Serves 4

Press the Sauté button on the multi-cooker and add the ghee to the pot. When melted, add the onion, beans, garlic and chilli/chile. Stir constantly for about 4–5 minutes. Then add the spices, salt and rice. Stir well. Add the spinach and 320 ml/11 fl. oz. water to the multi-cooker and deglaze the pot (see page 4).

Secure the lid in place and set to Rice for 12 minutes. At the end of cooking, use the QPR method (see page 4). Serve with strips of smoked salmon and quartered hard-boiled/cooked eggs on top.

COD IN PARMA HAM WITH LEMON BUTTER AND VEGETABLES

2 thick and chunky cod fillets
6 slices of Parma ham or prosciutto
1 tablespoon salted butter
½ head of cauliflower, chopped into medium florets
10 spears of asparagus, woody ends snapped off
3 mushrooms, halved
freshly squeezed juice of ½ lemon, plus lemon wedges to serve
1 tablespoon olive oil
salt and freshly ground black pepper

Serves 2

The ham combines deliciously with the buttery cod in this dish. It's a whole meal served with the vegetables that are all cooked in the pot at the same time.

Wrap each of the cod fillets in three slices of Parma or prosciutto ham.

Press the Sauté button on the multi-cooker. Add the butter and cauliflower and stir. When the butter begins to turn brown, add the asparagus and mushrooms and stir, then rest the ham-wrapped fish on top. Drizzle over the lemon juice and oil, then sprinkle over salt and pepper to taste.

Secure the lid in place and set to Manual or High Pressure for 2 minutes. At the end of cooking, use the QPR method (see page 4). Serve immediately, with lemon wedges on the side.

SMOKED HADDOCK WITH FENNEL AND MUSHROOMS

1 tablespoon olive oil
1 fennel bulb, very finely chopped (reserve the feathery fronds to garnish)
8 medium mushrooms, cut into quarters
10 cherry tomatoes, cut in half
2 chunky smoked haddock fillets
lemon wedges, to serve

Serves 2

A light, but flavoursome fish dish, and great for a quick and easy meal (photo on page 2).

Press the Sauté button on the multi-cooker and add the oil. When hot, add the fennel and stir for about 5 minutes until softened. Add the mushrooms and tomatoes and stir, then lay the fillets of fish on top.

Secure the lid in place and set to Manual or High Pressure for 1 minute. At the end of cooking, use the NPR method (see page 4). Serve with lemon wedges and garnish with chopped feathery fennel fronds.

ALL-IN-ONE SPAGHETTI BOLOGNESE

1½ tablespoons olive oil
2 small onions or 1 large onion, halved and thickly sliced
2 carrots, peeled, sliced into quarters lengthways and chopped into 1-cm/½-in. pieces
500 g/1 lb. 2 oz. organic minced/ground beef
10 chestnut mushrooms, halved
400 g/14 oz. passata/strained tomatoes
1 tablespoon tamari or coconut aminos
2 tablespoons tomato paste
1½ teaspoons dried oregano
1 vegetable stock cube or 1 tablespoon vegetable stock paste (see page 31)
150 g/5½ oz. wholegrain spelt spaghetti, snapped in half to ensure even cooking
grated Parmesan, to serve

Serves 4

This is one of those dishes that so many people love. Cooking the pasta in with the sauce is a real time-saver. This recipe uses wholegrain spelt spaghetti which adds great flavour.

Press the Sauté button on the multi-cooker and add the oil. When hot, add the onions and carrots. Stir for about 5 minutes until the onions become translucent. Add the beef and stir to break it up and ensure even cooking.

When the beef has browned, add the mushrooms, passata/strained tomatoes, tamari or coconut aminos, tomato paste, oregano and vegetable stock cube or paste, plus 300 ml/1¼ cups water. Deglaze the pot (see page 4), then push the halved spaghetti into the liquid, ensuring it is completely covered by the liquid.

Secure the lid in place and set to Manual or High Pressure for 7 minutes. At the end of cooking, use the QPR method (see page 4). Serve immediately, with grated Parmesan cheese if you wish.

BEEF BOLOGNESE

1½ tablespoons olive oil
2 small onions or 1 large onion, halved and thickly sliced
2 celery ribs/sticks, chopped into 1-cm/½-in. pieces
2 carrots, peeled, sliced into quarters lengthways and chopped into 1-cm/½-in. pieces
750 g/1 lb. 10 oz. organic minced/ground beef
10 chestnut mushrooms, halved
400 g/14 oz. passata/strained tomatoes
1 tablespoon tamari or coconut aminos
½ teaspoon salt
2 tablespoons tomato paste
1 tablespoon dried oregano

Serves 6

Beef bolognese can also be made as a sauce in the multi-cooker. If you prefer to cook the pasta separately or serve the bolognese over a vegetable-based pasta alternative, this is the vegetable-filled, flavour-packed bolognese sauce recipe you need.

Press the Sauté button on the multi-cooker and add the oil. When hot, add the onions, celery and carrots and stir until the onions become translucent. Next, add the beef and stir to break up any lumps. Once the beef has browned, add the mushrooms, passata/strained tomatoes, tamari or coconut aminos, salt, tomato paste and oregano. Stir to combine and deglaze the pot (see page 4).

Secure the lid in place and set to Manual or High Pressure for 15 minutes. At the end of cooking, use the NPR method (see page 4). Serve immediately.

PANCETTA AND TOMATO PASTA

1 tablespoon ghee or butter
1 onion, chopped
200 g/7 oz. diced pancetta or bacon
2 garlic cloves, crushed
1 tablespoon coconut aminos or tamari
1 courgette/zucchini, chopped
500 ml/2 cups vegetable stock
400 g/14 oz. passata/strained tomatoes
320 g/11 oz. brown rice fusilli
grated Parmesan, to serve

Serves 4

This is a really quick and easy meal made from straightforward ingredients.

Press the Sauté button on the multi-cooker and add the ghee or butter. When melted, add the onion and pancetta or bacon. Stir for about 3 minutes, then add the garlic and stir for another 2 minutes. Add the coconut aminos or tamari and deglaze the pot (see page 4), then add all the remaining ingredients and stir.

Secure the lid in place and set to Manual or High Pressure for 2 or 3 minutes (the pasta cooking time is reduced to one-third of the time stated on the package). At the end of cooking, use the QPR method (see page 4), open the lid and stir. Then leave the pasta in the pot until the desired consistency is reached. Serve sprinkled with grated Parmesan.

PEA AND PAPRIKA CREAMY PASTA

25 g/1/2 cup nutritional yeast flakes
1 1/2 teaspoons salt
1/2 teaspoon onion powder
1/2 teaspoon garlic powder
1/2 teaspoon smoked paprika
3 tablespoons olive oil
1 tablespoon freshly squeezed lemon juice
1 large sweet potato (about 400 g/14 oz.), peeled and cubed
4 medium tomatoes, chopped into wedges
250 g/9 oz. pea pasta
grated/shredded vegan cheese or sliced avocado, to serve

Serves 3

This pasta dish is 'creamy' and luxurious in taste. It's a delicious and nutritious vegan pasta dish.

In a bowl, mix together the nutritional yeast flakes, salt, onion powder, garlic powder and paprika. In a separate bowl mix together the olive oil and lemon juice.

Put the sweet potato cubes and tomato wedges into the multi-cooker. Add the nutritional yeast mixture and the olive oil mixture and stir. Add the pea pasta and 650 ml/2 3/4 cups water, then push all the pasta down into the water.

Secure the lid in place and set to Manual or High Pressure for 2 minutes. At the end of cooking, use the QPR method (see page 4). Serve with a sprinkling of vegan cheese or some sliced avocado.

BUTTERNUT SQUASH, CHORIZO AND ONION ON COURGETTI

1½ tablespoons olive oil
2 onions, cut into wedges
150 g/5½ oz. chorizo, thickly sliced
½ large butternut squash, peeled, deseeded and cut into large cubes
35 ml/2½ tablespoons coconut aminos or tamari
4 courgettes/zucchinis, made into courgetti using a spiralizer or julienne peeler (or a shop-bought bag of courgetti, available in most supermarkets)

Serves 2

For health reasons or allergy reasons, many people like to switch out wheat-based pasta for vegetable alternatives. This courgetti is a great addition to the combined flavours of chorizo and butternut squash and makes for a lower-carb but nutrient-rich meal for two.

Press the Sauté button on the multi-cooker and add the olive oil. When hot, add the onions to the pot and stir until nearly translucent. Add the chorizo and butternut squash and stir again. Add the coconut aminos or tamari and 2½ tablespoons water and stir again to deglaze the pot (see page 4).

Secure the lid in place and set to Manual or High Pressure for 3 minutes. At the end of cooking, use the QPR method (see page 4). Add the courgetti and stir to combine, then replace the lid and leave to 'mellow' for 2 minutes before serving.

SAUSAGE AND TOMATO SAUCE WITH COURGETTI

1 teaspoon olive oil
6 sausages, skins removed
1 tub of fresh pasta sauce (preferably tomato and basil)
4 courgettes/zucchinis, made into courgetti using a spiralizer or julienne peeler (or a shop-bought bag of courgetti, available in most supermarkets)

Serves 2

A ridiculously simple four-ingredient recipe, ideal for busy midweek evenings.

Press the Sauté button on the multi-cooker and add the olive oil, then crumble in the sausage meat. Break down the sausage meat with a wooden spoon until it resembles minced/ground meat in texture. Add the pasta sauce and stir.

Secure the lid in place and set to Manual or High Pressure for 4 minutes. At the end of cooking, use the QPR method (see page 4), then stir in the courgetti and let soften for a couple of minutes.

CHEESE-FILLED MEATBALLS IN A CHUNKY TOMATO SAUCE

FOR THE MEATBALLS

½ onion, very finely chopped
1 garlic clove, crushed
1 tablespoon barbecue sauce (ideally one with no added sugar)
1 tablespoon tomato paste
1 teaspoon Dijon mustard
1 teaspoon salt
800 g/1 lb. 12 oz. minced/ground beef
1 large egg or 1 duck egg
50 g/1 cup fresh breadcrumbs, gluten-free breadcrumbs or rice crumbs
100 g/1 cup finely grated Cheddar cheese

FOR THE SAUCE

1 teaspoon olive oil
½ onion, chopped
1 garlic clove, crushed
2 celery stalks, chopped
1 teaspoon salt
1 tablespoon balsamic vinegar
1 tablespoon tomato paste
1 x 400-g/14-oz. can chopped tomatoes
1 teaspoon dried oregano

Serves 4

These meatballs are what my children describe as 'comfort food'. Good served with spaghetti.

First, make the meatballs. Mix together the onion, garlic, barbecue sauce, tomato paste, mustard, salt, beef, egg and bread- or rice crumbs. Roll into about 15–17 balls, then flatten each one into a flat patty. Place a small mound of grated/shredded cheese in the centre of each, then close the meat up around the cheese to enclose it in a meatball.

To make the sauce, press the Sauté button on the multi-cooker and add the olive oil. When hot, add the onion, garlic and celery. Stir for a couple of minutes, then add the salt, vinegar and tomato paste and keep stirring for another few minutes. Next, add the tomatoes and deglaze the pan (see page 4), then stir in the oregano.

Place the meatballs in the sauce. Secure the lid in place and set to Manual or High Pressure for 20 minutes. At the end of cooking, use the NPR method (see page 4).

Note: if you prefer a smoother sauce, once cooked, remove the meatballs and process the sauce to a much smoother consistency before serving alongside/over the meatballs.

APRICOT TURKEY MEATBALLS

Light, fruity and flavoursome turkey meatballs.

1 x 400-g/14-oz. can apricot halves in natural juice, drained
30 g/1 oz. spring onions/scallions (white part only – use the green part as a garnish), very finely chopped
2 garlic cloves, crushed
1/4 teaspoon ground mace
1/4 teaspoon ground cinnamon
500 g/1 lb. 2 oz. minced/ground turkey
1/2 teaspoon salt
30 g/1/3 cup ground almonds
40 ml/2 1/2 tablespoons tamari or coconut aminos
1/2 teaspoon finely chopped fresh ginger
1/8 teaspoon ground nutmeg

Serves 4

Place the apricot halves in a food processor and process to a purée. Remove from the food processor and set aside. Put the spring onions/scallions, garlic, mace, cinnamon, turkey, salt and ground almonds in the food processor and process to combine. Roll the mixture into 12 equally-sized meatballs.

In the multi-cooker, mix 60 g/4 tablespoons apricot purée with the tamari or coconut aminos, ginger and nutmeg. Add the meatballs.

Secure the lid in place and set to Manual or High Pressure for 10 minutes. At the end of cooking, use the NPR method (see page 4).

To thicken the sauce, remove the meatballs and wrap in foil to keep warm. Press the Sauté button on the multi-cooker and stir the sauce until thickened. Serve the meatballs and sauce together, garnished with the chopped green spring onions/scallions.

MEATBALLS WITH LENTIL PASTA

These meatballs are moist and succulent thanks to the added vegetables. The lentil pasta makes this a very substantial dish for a family.

800 g/1 lb. 12 oz. minced/ground beef
2 eggs
1/2 courgette/zucchini, finely diced
1 carrot, finely diced
1 1/2 teaspoons salt
1 teaspoon dried oregano
50 g/4 tablespoons ground flaxseeds/linseeds
1 x 400-g/14-oz. can chopped tomatoes
2 tablespoons barbecue sauce (ideally one without added sugar)
1 tablespoon coconut aminos or tamari
1 vegetable stock cube or 1 tablespoon vegetable stock paste (see page 31)
250 g/9 oz. lentil pasta

Makes 20-22 meatballs/
Serves 6

In a bowl, mix together the beef, eggs, courgette/zucchini, carrot, salt, oregano and flaxseeds/linseeds. Form into meatballs about the size of large golf balls (this can get a little messy so I wear catering gloves).

Put the tomatoes, barbecue sauce, coconut aminos or tamari, stock cube or paste and 400 ml/1 2/3 cups water into the multi-cooker. Add the meatballs and push them under the sauce.

Secure the lid in place and set the Meat button for 12 minutes. At the end of cooking, use the NPR method (see page 4). Remove the meatballs and cover to keep warm.

Add the pasta to the pot. Secure the lid and cook on Manual or High Pressure for 2 minutes. At the end of cooking, use the QPR method (see page 4) and serve the pasta and meatballs together.

RICE AND GRAINS

COURGETTE, FETA AND MINT RISOTTO

2 tablespoons olive oil
2 small courgettes/zucchinis, chopped
1/4 teaspoon salt
2 onions, chopped
2 garlic cloves, crushed
75 ml/5 tablespoons dry white wine
250 g/2 1/4 cups Arborio rice
2 tablespoons vegetable stock paste (see page 31) or 2 vegetable stock cubes
150-g/5 1/2-oz. feta cheese, cubed
10 g/1/3 cup finely chopped fresh mint

Serves 6

This dish was created for a retreat I worked on in Corfu many years ago. A Sunday Times journalist on that particular trip raved about it and asked for the recipe, which she shared on her own travel blog. Including the recipe in this book was a no-brainer as the multi-cooker lends itself so well to risottos.

Press the Sauté button on the multi-cooker and add the oil. When hot, sauté the courgettes/zucchinis, sprinkling the salt over during sautéing. Remove to a bowl when coloured and soft. Add the onions to the pot. Cook for a few minutes, then add the garlic and wine and deglaze the pot (see page 4). Next, add the rice, stock paste/cubes and 600 ml/2 1/2 cups water and stir.

Secure the lid in place and set to Manual or High Pressure for 6 minutes. At the end of cooking, use the QPR method (see page 4) and stir in the cooked courgettes/zucchinis, feta and chopped mint. Good served with a green salad.

CASHEW NUT PILAFF

2 tablespoons olive oil or avocado oil
1 onion, very finely chopped or grated
1 garlic clove, crushed
1 carrot, grated
250 g/1 1/2 cups basmati rice, rinsed
1 teaspoon salt
1 teaspoon ground cumin
1 teaspoon ground coriander
1/2 teaspoon ground turmeric
100 g/3/4 cup roasted cashew nuts
2 tablespoons freshly chopped coriander/cilantro

Serves 4

Cashews lend a really sweet flavour and nutty texture to this pilaff. Make sure you add the fresh coriander/cilantro as this herb really makes this dish.

Press the Sauté button on the multi-cooker and add the oil. When hot, add the onion, garlic and carrot. Stir for about 5 minutes. Add the rice, salt and spices and stir well. Add 320 ml/1 1/3 cups water and deglaze the pan (see page 4).

Secure the lid in place and set to Rice for 12 minutes. At the end of cooking, use the QPR method (see page 4). Immediately stir in the cashew nuts and chopped coriander/cilantro and serve.

MUSHROOM RISOTTO

A creamy mushroom risotto made using classic ingredients.

1 tablespoon olive oil
1 large onion, finely chopped
3 garlic cloves, finely chopped
250 g/1⅓ cups Arborio rice
1 chicken or vegetable stock cube or 1 tablespoon vegetable stock paste (see page 31)
75 ml/5 tablespoons dry white wine, at room temperature
1 teaspoon salt
1 teaspoon dried thyme
200–250 g/7–9 oz. mixed mushrooms (including some Asian varieties), chopped into small pieces
freshly squeezed juice of ½ lemon
3 handfuls fresh spinach
55 g/½ cup grated/shredded mature Cheddar cheese
salt and freshly ground black pepper

Serves 4

Press the Sauté button on the multi-cooker and add the oil. When hot, sauté the onion and garlic for 3 minutes.

Add the rice and stir well. Add the stock cube or vegetable paste, 600 ml/2½ cups water, the wine, salt, thyme and mushrooms and stir once again to ensure the ingredients are thoroughly mixed.

Secure the lid in place and set to Manual or High Pressure for 6 minutes. At the end of cooking, use the QPR method (see page 4) to prevent the risotto from overcooking. Stir in the lemon juice, spinach, grated/shredded cheese and salt and pepper to taste. Stir well. If it's still a little too liquid, just let it sit for a couple of minutes as it will thicken as it cools. Serve with a mixed salad.

CHICKEN AND BACON RISOTTO

A very comforting meal achieved with minimal effort. The multi-cooker means there is no need to stand over the hob stirring constantly to create the perfect risotto.

1 tablespoon olive oil
1 onion, finely chopped
2 garlic cloves, crushed
4 slices of bacon, chopped
10 mushrooms, thickly sliced
500 g/1 lb. 2 oz. chicken, cut into cubes
150 ml/⅔ cup white wine
300 g/1⅔ cups Arborio rice
1 vegetable stock cube or 1 tablespoon vegetable stock paste (see page 31)
1 tablespoon freshly chopped thyme
1 tablespoon butter
grated pecorino or Parmesan cheese, to serve
freshly ground black pepper

Serves 4

Press the Sauté button on the multi-cooker and add the oil. When hot, add the onion, garlic, bacon, mushrooms and chicken and sauté for about 3 minutes. Add the wine to the pot to deglaze (see page 4). After a couple more minutes, stir in the rice, stock cube or paste, thyme and 600 ml/2½ cups water and stir really well.

Secure the lid in place and set to Rice for 12 minutes. At the end of cooking, use the QPR method (see page 4). Stir the risotto well to develop the creamy texture, then stir in the butter. Leave to stand for 3 minutes, then serve topped with Parmesan and freshly ground black pepper.

SPANISH RICE WITH MINCED PORK

75 g/1 cup finely grated Parmesan cheese
60 g/2 oz. chorizo, finely chopped
1 onion, ½ grated and ½ chopped
500 g/1 lb. 2 oz. minced/ground pork
1 tablespoon ghee
1 plump garlic clove, thinly sliced
2 carrots, chopped
1 tablespoon vegetable stock paste (see page 31) or 1 vegetable stock cube
1 teaspoon paprika
250 g/1½ cups basmati rice, rinsed
shavings of Manchego or Parmesan cheese, to serve

Serves 4

This family favourite combines the salty flavours of Parmesan and chorizo with mellow minced/ground pork and rice in a delicious meal.

In a food processor or by hand, mix the Parmesan, chorizo, grated onion and minced/ground pork.

Press the Sauté button on the multi-cooker and add the ghee. When hot, fry the chopped onion, garlic and carrots for 5 minutes, then add the pork mixture and stir, using a spoon to break up the mixture, until the pork is coloured. Add the stock paste or cube and stir, then add the paprika, rice and 320 ml/1⅓ cups water and deglaze the pan (see page 4).

Secure the lid in place and set to Rice for 12 minutes. At the end of cooking, use the QPR method (see page 4) and serve immediately with shavings of Manchego or Parmesan cheese on the top.

BUTTERNUT SQUASH AND CHORIZO GOLDEN RICE

310 g/11 oz. butternut squash, peeled, deseeded and cubed
115 g/4 oz. chorizo, cubed
250 g/1½ cups basamati rice, rinsed
2 tablespoons butter or ghee
salt and freshly ground black pepper

Serves 6 as a side dish

A deliciously buttery rice side dish that's a beautiful golden colour.

Place the butternut squash, chorizo, rice and 320 ml/11 fl. oz. water in the multi-cooker.

Secure the lid in place and set to Rice for 12 minutes. At the end of cooking, use the QPR method (see page 4) and open the lid. Stir in the butter or ghee and the seasoning, then serve.

SPEEDY VEGETABLE BIRYANI

2 tablespoons butter, ghee, avocado oil or olive oil
1 onion, coarsely grated
1 carrot, coarsely grated
1 courgette/zucchini, coarsely grated
2 garlic cloves, finely grated
10 mushrooms, thickly sliced
250 g/1½ cups basmati rice, rinsed
1 teaspoon salt
¾ teaspoon ground cumin
½ teaspoon ground turmeric

Serves 4

This is our family's favourite rice dish. It can be enjoyed alone, with other Indian veggie dishes or even eaten cold as part of a buffet or packed lunch the next day.

Press the Sauté button on the multi-cooker and add the butter, ghee or oil. When melted or hot, add the onion, carrot, courgette/zucchini, garlic and mushrooms. Stir for about 5 minutes. Add the rice, salt and spices and stir well. Add 320 ml/1⅓ cups water and deglaze the pan (see page 4).

Secure the lid in place and set to Rice for 12 minutes. At the end of cooking, use the QPR method (see page 4), then serve.

PEA AND CORN RICE

2 tablespoons olive oil
1 large onion, chopped
¼ teaspoon salt
2 tablespoons freshly chopped coriander/cilantro
2 garlic cloves, crushed
1 teaspoon ground turmeric
125 g/4½ oz. canned or frozen sweetcorn/corn kernels
150 g/1¼ cups frozen peas
250 g/1½ cups basmati rice, rinsed
1 tablespoon vegetable stock paste (see page 31) or 1 vegetable stock cube
2 tablespoons butter or ghee, or olive oil for a vegan dish

Serves 4 as a side dish

This is one of the simplest rice dishes but it's a great dish for those who love peas and corn. In my work as a nutritionist I've met so many people who tell me these are their favourite two vegetables. Pea and sweetcorn lovers, this dish is for you!

Press the Sauté button on the multi-cooker and add the olive oil. When hot, add the onion and sprinkle with the salt. Cook for about 5 minutes, stirring regularly. Add the coriander/cilantro, garlic and turmeric and stir again, then add the sweetcorn, peas and rice. Stir once again, then add 320 ml/1⅓ cups water and the stock paste or cube, then deglaze the pan (see page 4).

Secure the lid in place and set to Rice for 12 minutes. At the end of cooking, use the QPR method (see page 4). Stir in the butter, ghee or oil and serve.

MEDITERRANEAN CHICKEN WITH RICE

1 tablespoon ghee
1 onion, chopped
2 garlic cloves, crushed
2 teaspoons smoked paprika
3/4 teaspoon salt
4 tomatoes, quartered
2 chicken breasts, sliced
approx. 20 French/green beans, topped, tailed and chopped into 1-cm/1/2-in. lengths
250 g/1 1/2 cups basmati rice, rinsed
1 chicken stock cube or 1 tablespoon vegetable stock paste (see page 31)
24 pitted/stoned black olives
1 pot of marinated artichokes
4 slices of Parma ham or prosciutto, torn roughly

Serves 4

This is a very simple chicken and rice dish. It's a great meal to put together if you have unexpected guests for dinner.

Press the Sauté button on the multi-cooker and add the ghee. When melted, add the onion and garlic and stir constantly for about 4 minutes. Then add the paprika, salt, tomatoes, chicken and French/green beans and stir. Stir in the rice, then add 320 ml/11 fl. oz. water and the stock cube or paste.

Secure the lid in place and set to Rice for 12 minutes. At the end of cooking, use the QPR method (see page 4). Stir in the olives, artichokes and torn Parma ham or prosciutto. Serve immediately.

QUINOA PILAFF

1 tablespoon butter or avocado oil
1 onion, chopped
½ green chilli/chile, chopped
3 carrots, finely chopped
1 teaspoon freshly grated ginger
3 garlic cloves, crushed
140 g/5 oz. frozen spinach
85 g/¾ cup frozen peas
170 g/1 cup quinoa
1 teaspoon salt

Serves 4

Quinoa is known as a pseudo-grain. It's actually closely related to beetroot/beet and spinach. It provides a nutrient-dense base ingredient for this pilaff.

Press the Sauté button on the multi-cooker and add the butter or oil. When hot, add the onion, chilli/chile, carrots, ginger and garlic and stir until the onion is almost transparent. Add the spinach and peas and stir once more. Then add the quinoa, salt and 230 ml/ 1 cup water, giving the pot a final stir.

Secure the lid in place and set to Manual or High Pressure for 2 minutes. At the end of cooking, use the NPR method (see page 4).

MUSHROOM QUIN-OTTO

2 tablespoons avocado oil, olive oil or butter
1 onion, finely chopped
20 g/¾ oz. dried shiitake mushrooms or mixed dried mushrooms, soaked in water for as long as it says on the packaging (reserve the soaking water)
3 garlic cloves, crushed
170 g/1 cup quinoa, rinsed
½ teaspoon salt
½ teaspoon freshly ground black pepper
1 teaspoon dried thyme
2 tablespoons grated Parmesan, pecorino or vegan cheese

Serves 4 as a main meal with a side salad

This is like a mushroom risotto but made using quinoa rather than rice. Use oil and vegan cheese to make this purely vegan.

Press the Sauté button on the multi-cooker and add the oil or butter. When hot, add the onion and cook for 5 minutes. Add the mushrooms, garlic, quinoa, salt, pepper and thyme plus 250 ml/ 1 cup of the mushroom soaking water and stir to deglaze the pot (see page 4).

Secure the lid in place and set to Manual or High Pressure for 2 minutes. At the end of cooking, use the QPR method (see page 4) and stir the cheese into the quin-otto before you serve.

CURRIES AND CHILLIES

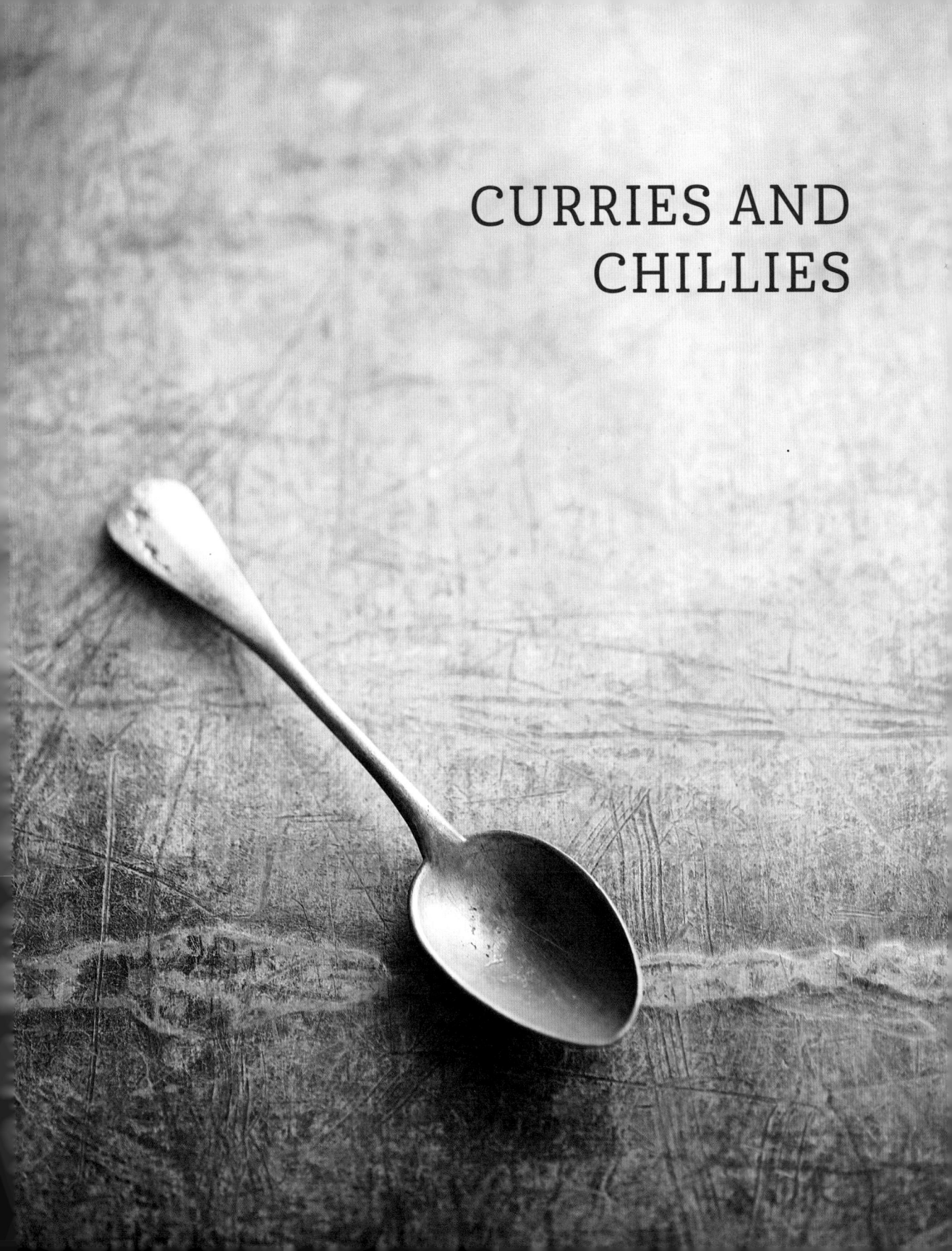

CHICKEN TIKKA MASALA

2 onions, chopped
1 garlic clove, crushed
1-cm/½-in. piece of fresh ginger, grated
2 teaspoons garam masala
¾ teaspoon paprika
¾ teaspoon ground turmeric
1 teaspoon ground cumin
½ teaspoon ground cinnamon
2 teaspoons salt
500-g/18-oz. can passata/strained tomatoes
450 g/1 lb. boneless chicken breasts, cut into bite-sized pieces
½ x 400-g/14-oz. can coconut milk (ideally the thick, creamy part of it which has separated)

Serves 4

No take-out curry order would be complete without ordering this dish, yet it can be made in minutes in your own home using very straightforward ingredients.

Put all the ingredients except the coconut milk into the multi-cooker, making sure the chicken goes in last so it doesn't stick to the bottom during cooking.

Secure the lid in place and set to Poultry for 15 minutes. At the end of cooking, use the QPR method (see page 4). Add the coconut milk, stir and keep warm in the pot until ready to serve. Serve the curry on Cauliflower Rice (see page 85) or basmati rice.

ALMOND SATAY

50 g/2 oz. chopped peeled sweet potato
75 g/2¾ oz. French/green beans
2 boneless chicken breasts, sliced into mini fillets
5 drops of fish sauce
1 teaspoon freshly grated ginger
1 teaspoon tamari or coconut aminos
80 g/5½ tablespoons almond butter
200 ml/¾ cup coconut milk

Serves 2

This is a rich and 'creamy' dairy-free dish. Satay is, of course, traditionally made using peanut butter or ground peanuts, but as almonds are more nutritious and simply delicious, I've used them instead.

Place the vegetables and chicken pieces in the multi-cooker. In a bowl, mix together the fish sauce, grated ginger, tamari or coconut aminos, almond butter and coconut milk. (If the almond butter is fridge-hard, you may need to soften it a little by mixing with a drop of warm water before adding it to the sauce.) Pour the sauce into the pot and stir to mix.

Secure the lid in place and set to Manual or High Pressure for 3 minutes. At the end of cooking, use the NPR method (see page 4).

BEEF MASSAMAN WITH NEW POTATOES

1 tablespoon ghee
2 onions, sliced
2 carrots, chopped
500 g/1 lb. 2 oz. minced/ground beef
2 tablespoons massaman curry paste
1½ teaspoons tamari or coconut aminos
¼ teaspoon fish sauce
100 ml/6 tablespoons coconut milk
350 g/12 oz. new potatoes, cut in half
freshly chopped coriander/cilantro, to garnish

Serves 3–4

This is a simply delicious, all-in-one mid-week meal. This Thai-style curry is mild and full of authentic flavour.

Press the Sauté button on the multi-cooker and add the ghee. When melted, add the onions and carrots and sauté for a few minutes. Add the beef and break it up to allow even browning. Add the curry paste, tamari or coconut aminos, fish sauce and coconut milk, then stir to deglaze the pot (see page 4).

Secure the lid in place and set to Manual or High Pressure for 10 minutes. At the end of cooking use the QPR method (see page 4).

Add the potatoes to the pot. Secure the lid in place and set to Manual or High Pressure for 4 minutes. At the end of cooking, use the NPR method (see page 4). Garnish with coriander/cilantro.

RED THAI BEEF CURRY

1 tablespoon ghee
2 onions, each sliced into 8 wedges
2 garlic cloves, thinly sliced
900 g/2 lb. casserole/stewing beef, cubed
1 tablespoon Thai red curry paste (ideally one without added sugar)
1 teaspoon fish sauce
1 teaspoon salt
1 teaspoon coconut sugar
1 teaspoon balsamic vinegar
1 teaspoon tamari or coconut aminos
200 ml/¾ cup thick coconut milk
2 sweet potatoes, peeled, halved and chopped into large chunks
300 g/10½ oz. fresh spinach
4 tablespoons coconut yogurt or soured/sour cream, to serve
freshly chopped coriander/cilantro, to garnish

Serves 6

What's not to love about a Thai curry? This one has a vibrant and appealing colour and, with only a small amount of spice, won't deter spice-detecting palates.

Press the Sauté button on the multi-cooker and add the ghee. When melted, add the onions and garlic and cook, stirring with a wooden spoon, for about 5 minutes. Next, add the beef and stir to ensure the outside of most pieces is browned. Add the curry paste, fish sauce, salt, coconut sugar, balsamic vinegar and tamari or coconut aminos and deglaze the pot (see page 4). Add the coconut milk and sweet potatoes and give one more stir.

Secure the lid in place and set to Manual or High Pressure for 25 minutes. At the end of cooking, use the NPR method (see page 4). Open the lid and add in the spinach, stirring until all the leaves have wilted. Serve with coconut yogurt or soured/sour cream on top and a scattering of freshly chopped coriander/cilantro.

AROMATIC PANEER CURRY

1 onion, chopped
3 tomatoes, cut into quarters
5 baby aubergines/eggplants, cut into quarters (or 1 large aubergine/eggplant chopped into 2 x 2-cm/¾ x ¾-in. pieces)
1 green chilli/chile, finely chopped
1 teaspoon freshly grated ginger
2 tablespoons ghee
2 sprigs of fresh curry leaves (optional)
1 tablespoon freshly chopped coriander/cilantro
½ teaspoon date syrup or maple syrup
½ teaspoon salt
4 teaspoons korma paste
2 teaspoons avocado oil or olive oil
500 g/1 lb. 2 oz. paneer, cubed

Serves 4

Paneer cheese has a delicious texture – it's a little bit like halloumi but softer. It makes for a great vegetarian curry.

Place the onion, tomatoes, aubergines/eggplants, chilli/chile, ginger, ghee, curry leaves, coriander/cilantro, date or maple syrup, salt and 80 ml/5½ tablespoons water in the multi-cooker. Secure the lid in place and set to Manual or High Pressure for 10 minutes.

Meanwhile, mix the korma paste and oil together in a large bowl and tip in the paneer cubes. Toss the paneer with your hands or a spoon to coat.

When the curry sauce is cooked, use the QPR method (see page 4). Remove the curry leaves. Using a stick blender or food processor, blend the contents of the inner pot. Press the Sauté button and allow the sauce to bubble for 5 minutes, then add the korma-coated paneer. Cook for a further 5 minutes, then serve.

VEGETABLE CURRY

1 tablespoon ghee, butter or avocado oil
1 onion, chopped
1 teaspoon freshly grated ginger
1 small green chilli/chile, finely chopped
2 carrots, chopped
1 teaspoon ground cumin
½ teaspoon ground turmeric
¼ teaspoon chilli/chili powder
1 heaped teaspoon salt
1 small cauliflower, chopped into large florets
2 tomatoes, cut into eighths
160 ml/⅔ cup canned coconut cream

Serves 4

A simple veggie curry – simple ingredients and simple to make.

Press the Sauté button on the multi-cooker and add the ghee, butter or oil. When hot, add the onion, ginger, chilli/chile and carrots. Stir until the onion is just becoming translucent. Add the spices and salt and stir well, then stir in the cauliflower florets and tomatoes. Add the coconut cream and give everything one last stir to deglaze the pan (see page 4).

Secure the lid in place and set to Manual or High Pressure for 2 minutes. At the end of cooking, use the QPR method (see page 4) and serve.

SAAG (INDIAN SPINACH)

1 tablespoon ghee or avocado oil
1 onion, chopped
2 garlic cloves, crushed
2.5 x 5-cm/1 x 2-in. piece of fresh ginger, peeled and grated
3/4 teaspoon salt
1/2 teaspoon ground coriander
1/4 teaspoon ground turmeric
1/2 teaspoon ground cumin
1/2 teaspoon mustard powder
500 g/1 lb. 2 oz. frozen spinach (in cubes)

Serves 4 as a side dish

A delightfully aromatic Indian side dish. It's a great accompaniment to many of the rice dishes in this book.

Press the Sauté button on the multi-cooker and add the ghee or oil. When hot, add the onion. Stir until translucent, then add the garlic and ginger and stir briefly, then add all the remaining ingredients and 3 tablespoons water.

Secure the lid in place and set to Manual or High Pressure for 4 minutes. At the end of cooking, use the QPR method (see page 4). Open the pot and stir, then serve with naan or hot dosa.

SAG ALOO (SPINACH AND POTATO CURRY)

2 tablespoons butter, ghee, avocado oil or olive oil
1 onion, chopped
560 g/1 lb. 4 oz. potatoes, peeled and chopped
1/2 red chilli/chile, deseeded and chopped
300 g/10 1/2 oz. frozen spinach
2 garlic cloves, sliced
1 tablespoon freshly grated ginger
1 teaspoon salt
1/2 teaspoon ground turmeric
1/2 teaspoon ground cumin
1/2 teaspoon nigella/black onion seeds

Serves 4 as a side dish

A curry take-away favourite for many, this spinach and potato dish can work as a standalone curry but it's even better served alongside another vegetable curry.

Press the Sauté button on the multi-cooker and add the butter, ghee or oil. When hot, add the onion, potatoes, chilli/chile and spinach. Stir for about 5 minutes, then add the garlic, ginger, salt and spices and 200 ml/3/4 cup water and stir to deglaze the pan (see page 4).

Secure the lid in place and set to Manual or High Pressure for 3 minutes. At the end of cooking, use the QPR method (see page 4), then serve.

THAI CHICKEN WITH CAULIFLOWER RICE

- 1 tablespoon butter
- 1 teaspoon olive oil
- 1 large cauliflower, chopped into florets, then processed to a 'rice' consistency in a food processor (alternatively, buy a supermarket packet of prepared cauliflower 'rice')
- 2 garlic cloves, crushed
- 2 sweet potatoes, peeled and chopped
- 25 French/green beans, topped and tailed (fresh or frozen)
- 1½ teaspoons Thai blend of dry spices
- 2 tablespoons tamari or coconut aminos
- 1 teaspoon fish sauce
- 1 teaspoon freshly grated ginger
- 1 x 400-ml/14-fl. oz. can coconut milk
- 4 boneless chicken breasts, sliced

Serves 4

An aromatic Thai curry served with low-carbohydrate cauliflower rice.

Press the Sauté button on the multi-cooker and add the butter and oil. When hot, add the cauliflower rice and stir constantly for about 5 minutes until the rice is just coloured. Remove from the pot, place in a warm bowl and cover with foil to keep warm.

Add all the remaining ingredients to the pot. Secure the lid in place and set to Manual or High Pressure for 3 minutes. At the end of cooking, use the QPR method (see page 4). Serve over the cauliflower rice.

MALAYSIAN CHICKEN

- 1 teaspoon ghee
- 2 onions, roughly chopped
- 1 large garlic clove, chopped
- 6 boneless chicken breasts
- 2 teaspoons Malaysian spice mix
- 1½ tablespoons tamari or coconut aminos
- 1½ teaspoons fish sauce
- 300 ml/1¼ cups canned coconut milk
- 15–20 mangetout/snow peas

Serves 6

Malaysian flavours are subtle and aromatic in this easy-to-make curry dish.

Press the Sauté button on the multi-cooker and add the ghee. When hot, add the onions and sauté for 5 minutes, then add the garlic and chicken. Seal the chicken all over, then add the spice, tamari or coconut aminos, fish sauce and coconut milk and deglaze the pot (see page 4).

Secure the lid in place and set to Manual or High Pressure for 12 minutes. At the end of cooking, use the NPR method (see page 4). Open the lid and stir in the mangetout/snow peas. Allow to cook in the residual heat for up to 5 minutes, then serve. Delicious over roasted turmeric cauliflower or with butternut squash 'spaghetti'.

MILD BUTTERNUT DHAL

1 onion
3 celery stalks
10 g/4 tablespoons freshly chopped coriander/cilantro
180 g/6½ oz. butternut squash
1 tablespoon olive oil
3 tablespoons tomato paste
1 teaspoon garlic powder
1½ tablespoons mild curry powder
160 g/1 cup split red lentils, washed thoroughly
1 tablespoon vegetable stock paste (see page 31) or 1 vegetable stock cube
freshly squeezed lemon juice (up to ½ lemon)
salt and freshly ground black pepper

Serves 4

Partnering sweet butternut squash with the dense texture of cooked lentils really makes this dhal stand out. The addition of lemon juice makes it sparkle even more.

Very finely chop the onion, celery, coriander/cilantro and butternut squash. (Using a food processor at this stage will save you a lot of time.)

Press the Sauté button on the multi-cooker and add the olive oil. When hot, add the finely chopped vegetables to the pot and stir until the onion becomes translucent. Add the tomato paste, garlic powder and curry powder and stir well. Add the lentils, stock paste or cube and 750 ml/3 cups water and deglaze the pan (see page 4).

Secure the lid in place and set to Manual or High Pressure for 3 minutes. At the end of cooking, use the NPR method (see page 4) for 15 minutes, then release the rest of the pressure using the QPR method. Serve with added lemon juice and salt and pepper to taste.

CHANA MASALA QUINOA

1 tablespoon olive oil or avocado oil
1 teaspoon cumin seeds
1 onion, chopped
2 garlic cloves, finely chopped
1 tablespoon finely chopped fresh ginger
1 small chilli/chile, finely chopped (omit this if serving to children who don't like the heat)
1 teaspoon garam masala
¾ teaspoon ground coriander
½ teaspoon ground turmeric
1 teaspoon salt
170 g/1 cup quinoa
135 g/5 oz. passata/strained tomatoes
1 x 400-g/14-oz. can chickpeas, drained
lime pickle, to serve

Serves 3

Chickpeas feature widely in Asian cuisine. They absorb flavour so well, as in this dish of chickpeas and quinoa combined with Asian spices. A pickle served with the dish works wonderfully.

Press the Sauté button on the multi-cooker and add the oil. When hot, add the cumin seeds and stir until fragrant, then add the onion and stir. Next add the garlic and ginger and stir, then add the other spices, salt and quinoa. Add the passata and 125 ml/8 tablespoons water to the pot. Deglaze the pan (see page 4).

Secure the lid in place and set to Manual or High Pressure for 2 minutes. At the end of cooking, use the QPR method (see page 4). Stir in the chickpeas and leave to warm through, then serve with lime pickle.

LAMB SAAG

1 teaspoon cumin seeds
1 teaspoon coriander seeds
1 onion
2-cm/3/4-in. piece of fresh ginger
2 plump garlic cloves, peeled
2 tablespoons freshly chopped coriander/cilantro
1 tablespoon ghee
450 g/1 lb. boneless lamb, cubed
4 tomatoes, quartered
2 cardamom pods
3/4 teaspoon ground turmeric
1 teaspoon salt
230 g/4 cups baby spinach leaves, rinsed

Serves 2–3

This is delicious served with Speedy Vegetable Biryani (see page 68).

Press the Sauté button on the multi-cooker. Put the cumin and coriander seeds in the pot. Once you start to smell the aroma from the seeds, transfer them to a food processor. Add the onion, ginger, garlic and coriander/cilantro and chop finely.

Add the ghee to the pot. When melted, add the contents of the food processor. Stir for about 3 minutes, then add the lamb and brown on all sides. Add the tomatoes, cardamom, turmeric and salt and stir. Add 125 ml/8 tablespoons water and stir.

Secure the lid in place and set to Meat/Stew for 35 minutes. At the end of cooking, use the NPR method (see page 4). Stir in the spinach before serving.

GREEN BEAN AND CAULIFLOWER CURRY

90 g/3¼ oz. frozen French/green beans
500 g/1 lb. 2 oz. cauliflower, cut into large florets
1 onion, finely chopped
2 tomatoes, chopped
2 carrots, chopped
150 ml/⅔ cup coconut milk
1 teaspoon salt
1 teaspoon vegetable stock paste (see page 31)
1½ teaspoons medium curry powder
1 teaspoon freshly grated ginger
freshly chopped coriander/cilantro, to garnish

Serves 4

This is a very simple curry recipe that's great for using up vegetables. It's very quick to make, too, so one for those evenings when you are too tired to think.

Put all the vegetables in the multi-cooker. In a bowl, mix together the coconut milk, salt, stock paste, curry powder and ginger. Add this mixture to the pot and stir.

Secure the lid in place and set to Manual or High Pressure for 1 minute. At the end of cooking, use the QPR method (see page 4). Serve with coriander/cilantro sprinkled over the top.

AUBERGINE AND CAULIFLOWER CURRY

1 teaspoon yellow mustard seeds
2 tablespoons avocado oil or olive oil
2 onions, chopped
2 garlic cloves, crushed or grated
1 teaspoon freshly grated ginger
2 medium aubergines/eggplants, chopped into 3 x 3-cm/1¼ x 1¼-in. pieces
1 large cauliflower, chopped into large florets
1 x 400-g/14-oz. can crushed tomatoes
1 teaspoon salt
1 x 400-g/14-oz. can chickpeas, drained and rinsed
2 tablespoons curry powder
natural/plain yogurt and freshly chopped coriander/cilantro, to serve

Serves 4

This is an option for a busy weekday evening as it uses mostly storecupboard ingredients and doesn't need much planning. It goes well with Speedy Vegetable Biriyani (see page 68).

Press the Sauté button on the multi-cooker. Add the mustard seeds and dry-fry until they darken in colour. Remove from the pot and discard. Add the oil to the pot and when hot, add the onions, garlic and ginger, stirring until the onions start to soften. Add the aubergines/eggplants and cauliflower and stir. Add the crushed tomatoes, salt, chickpeas, curry powder and 110 ml/½ cup water and deglaze the pot (see page 4).

Secure the lid in place and set to Manual or High Pressure for 3 minutes. At the end of cooking, use the NPR method (see page 4). Serve with a dollop of plain yogurt and a sprinkling of fresh coriander/cilantro.

AUBERGINE AND WHITE SWEET POTATO BHAJI CURRY

3 tablespoons olive oil, avocado oil, butter or ghee
1 onion, chopped
6 baby aubergines/eggplants, cut into quarters
2 white sweet potatoes, peeled and chopped
2 garlic cloves, grated
3-cm/1¼-in. piece of fresh ginger, grated
1 teaspoon salt
1 teaspoon garam masala
1 teaspoon ground cumin
6 cherry tomatoes, halved

Serves 4

Soft, succulent aubergines/eggplants combine with the mellow flavour of white sweet potato in this delicious veggie curry.

Press the Sauté button on the multi-cooker and add the oil, butter or ghee. Once hot or melted, add the onion, aubergines/eggplants and sweet potatoes. Stir for about 7 minutes, then add the garlic and ginger with the salt and spices and stir again. Finally, add the cherry tomatoes and 70 ml/5 tablespoons water and deglaze the pan (see page 4).

Secure the lid in place and set to Manual or High Pressure for 2 minutes. At the end of cooking, use the QPR method (see page 4).

MILD CHILLI BEEF WITH SWEET POTATO AND BLACK BEANS

1 tablespoon olive oil
2 onions, chopped
500 g/1 lb. 2 oz. minced/ground beef
½ teaspoon cumin seeds
¼ teaspoon mild chilli/chili powder
½ teaspoon ground coriander
½ teaspoon smoked paprika
2 garlic cloves, chopped
3 tablespoons tomato paste
1 stock cube or 1 tablespoon vegetable stock paste (see page 31)
1 large sweet potato, peeled and chopped
1 x 400-g/14-oz. can chopped tomatoes
1 x 400-g/14-oz. can black beans, drained and rinsed
soured/sour cream and guacamole, to serve

Serves 4

This is a mild chilli ideal for anyone sensitive to spice and heat. Kidney beans are replaced by black beans as they have a slightly sweeter taste, which may appeal to younger diners.

Press the Sauté button on the multi-cooker and add the oil. When hot, add the onions and stir for 4 minutes. Add the beef, cumin seeds, chilli/chili powder, coriander and paprika and stir again, ensuring the bottom of the pan is deglazed (see page 4). Once the beef is brown, add the garlic, tomato paste and stock cube or paste and 140 ml/⅔ cup water and deglaze again. Add the sweet potato and canned tomatoes.

Secure the lid in place and set to Manual or High Pressure for 15 minutes. At the end of cooking, use the QPR method (see page 4), then press Sauté, add the black beans and stir. Serve the after 5 minutes, with a dollop of sour/soured cream and guacamole on top.

CHILLI BEEF AND MUSHROOMS

1 tablespoon ghee
1 large onion, sliced
3 garlic cloves, chopped
500 g/1 lb. 2 oz. minced/ground beef
1 tablespoon balsamic vinegar
1 tablespoon tamari or coconut aminos
1 teaspoon coconut sugar
2 teaspoons chilli/chili powder
1 teaspoon ground cumin
1/4 teaspoon ground cinnamon
3 allspice berries
3 tablespoons tomato paste
200 g/7 oz. button mushrooms, cleaned but left whole
sliced avocado and soured/sour cream, to serve

Serves 4

This dish is all about umami, our fifth taste. It's packed full of flavour and texture, from the melt-in-the-mouth mushrooms to the strong flavours of balsamic vinegar, tamari and coconut.

Press the Sauté button on the multi-cooker and add the ghee. When hot, add the onion and garlic and stir. After 3 minutes, add the beef and break it up with a wooden spoon. Once browned, add the balsamic vinegar, tamari or coconut aminos, sugar, chilli/chili powder, cumin, cinnamon, allspice berries and tomato paste and stir to deglaze the pot (see page 4). Finally, stir in the mushrooms.

Secure the lid in place and set to Manual or High Pressure for 10 minutes. At the end of cooking, use the NPR method (see page 4). Serve in deep bowls with sliced avocado and soured/sour cream.

SPICY MINCED PORK

1 1/2 teaspoons olive oil
1 onion, chopped
2 carrots, diced into 1 x 1-cm/1/2 x 1/2-in. pieces
1 courgette/zucchini, diced into 2 x 2-cm/3/4 x 3/4-in. pieces
1 garlic clove, finely chopped
500 g/1 lb. 2 oz. minced/ground pork
1 tablespoon tomato paste
1 teaspoon smoked paprika
1 teaspoon coconut sugar
3/4 teaspoon salt
200 g/7 oz. canned cherry tomatoes
150 g/5 1/2 oz. mushrooms, cut into quarters
1 teaspoon dried oregano
sliced avocado and soured/sour cream, to serve

Serves 4

Pork, paprika and tomato are simply made for one another. These delicious flavours combine in this sumptuous spicy pork dish.

Press the Sauté button on the multi-cooker and add the oil. When hot, add the onion, carrots and courgette/zucchini and sauté until the onion is translucent. Add the garlic and pork and stir, breaking up the meat with a spoon, until the pork has browned. Add the tomato paste, paprika, coconut sugar, salt and tomatoes and stir again, being sure to deglaze the pot (see page 4). Add the mushrooms and oregano and give the mix one last stir.

Secure the lid in place and set to Manual or High Pressure for 15 minutes. At the end of cooking, use the NPR method (see page 4). Serve with sliced avocado and a dollop of soured/sour cream on top.

CASSEROLES AND ROASTS

LAMB RACK STEW

3½ tablespoons red wine
1 tablespoon tomato paste
1 tablespoon barbecue sauce (ideally one with no added sugar)
1 teaspoon smoked paprika
1 tablespoon tamari or coconut aminos
½ teaspoon garlic powder
a pinch of dried rosemary
1 teaspoon salt
4 celery stalks, cut into 5-cm/2-in. lengths
4 carrots, cut into 3-cm/1¼-in. lengths
3 tomatoes, cut into quarters
650 g/1 lb. 7 oz. rack of lamb, cut in half

Serves 2

This stew is characterized by the tenderness of the lamb, which is literally falling off the bone when it is served. This stew is so comforting and full of delicious ingredients that just work so well together.

Place all the ingredients apart from the lamb rack in the multi-cooker, add 150 ml/⅔ cup water and stir. Add the lamb rack.

Secure the lid in place and set to Manual or High Pressure for 30 minutes. At the end of cooking, use the NPR method (see page 4) and then serve.

LAMB TAGINE

¾ teaspoon ground cinnamon
¾ teaspoon ground turmeric
¾ teaspoon ground ginger
1 teaspoon ground cumin
1 teaspoon salt
2 tablespoons date nectar or honey
2 tablespoons olive oil, plus 1 tablespoon for cooking
800 g/1 lb. 12 oz. lamb shoulder, diced
1 onion, chopped
2 garlic cloves, sliced
6 organic dried apricots, sliced
2 sweet potatoes, peeled and chopped
a handful of toasted flaked/slivered almond

Serves 6

This dish has the taste and smell of a souk in Marrakesh. It's so aromatic, yet uses everyday spices.

In a small bowl or ramekin, make a paste from the spices, salt, date nectar or honey and 2 tablespoons of the olive oil. Place the diced lamb in a large bowl, add the spice paste and stir to coat the lamb.

Press the Sauté button on the multi-cooker and add the remaining 1 tablespoon olive oil. When hot, add the onion and garlic and stir rapidly for 4 minutes, then add the paste-coated lamb and keep stirring. After another 3 minutes, add the apricots and sweet potatoes.

Secure the lid in place and set to Stew for 20 minutes. At the end of cooking, use the NPR method (see page 4). Serve each bowlful with some toasted flaked/slivered almond scattered over the top. This tagine is good served with couscous.

MOROCCAN LAMB

1 tablespoon avocado oil or ghee
400 g/14 oz. soffrito (a mix of carrot, celery and onion, chopped and ready to cook)
3 tablespoons harissa paste
2 teaspoons salt
2 tablespoons tomato paste
800 g/1 lb. 12 oz. minced/ground lamb
2 sweet potatoes, peeled and chopped
sliced avocado, to serve

Serves 4

This is one of those meals you'll be extremely grateful for during busy times. It takes very little time to prepare, especially if you buy a pack of ready-chopped vegetables, and the result tastes fabulous.

Put everything apart from the sliced avocado into the multi-cooker and stir. Secure the lid in place and set to Manual or High Pressure for 18 minutes. At the end of cooking, use the NPR method (see page 4). Serve in bowls with sliced avocado on top.

SEAFOOD STEW

500 g/1 lb. 2 oz. skinless halibut or cod fillets, cut into bite-sized pieces
1 teaspoon freshly squeezed lime juice
1 tablespoon ghee or butter
1 onion, chopped
1 garlic clove, crushed
1 courgette/zucchini, thickly sliced
1 x 200-g/7-oz. can chopped tomatoes
250 ml/1 cup coconut milk
1 teaspoon salt
250 g/9 oz. raw king prawns/shrimp, peeled
freshly chopped parsley, to garnish
lemon wedges, to serve

Serves 4

Fish dishes are often some of the tastiest due to the sauce the fish is served in. The multi-cooker can make great-tasting sauces in a short period of time, and fish that needs very little cooking can be added at the end of pressure cooking so it is just soft and flaking when you eat the dish.

Place the fish in a shallow dish and squeeze or drizzle over the lime juice, then toss the fish with your hands to coat each piece. Set aside.

Press the Sauté button on the multi-cooker and add the ghee or butter. When melted, add the onion and stir for about 5 minutes. Add the garlic, courgette/zucchini, chopped tomatoes, coconut milk and salt.

Secure the lid in place and set to Manual or High Pressure for 5 minutes. At the end of cooking, use the QPR method (see page 4). Add the fish and the prawns/shrimp to the dish and stir. Set the multi-cooker to Keep Warm until they are just cooked. Serve immediately, garnished with parsley and with lemon wedges on the side.

CHICKEN CACCIATORE

1 tablespoon olive oil
1 onion, roughly chopped
2 celery stalks, roughly chopped
4 slices of bacon, cut into thin strips
1 garlic clove, chopped
400 g/14 oz. mini chicken fillets
1 teaspoon coconut sugar
1 teaspoon salt
1 tablespoon tomato paste
1 teaspoon dried rosemary
6 mushrooms, cut into quarters
1 x 400-g/14-oz. can chopped tomatoes
20 pitted/stoned black olives

Serves 4

Succulent chicken fillets combine with salty bacon and fruity tomatoes in this delicious Italian classic.

Press the Sauté button on the multi-cooker and add the oil. When hot, add the onion and celery and stir for 3 minutes, then add the bacon and garlic and stir for another 2 minutes. Add the chicken and stir for another 3 minutes. Add the coconut sugar, salt, tomato paste, rosemary, mushrooms, tomatoes and black olives.

Secure the lid in place and set to Manual or High Pressure for 7 minutes. At the end of cooking, use the NPR method (see page 4) and serve immediately.

CAJUN CHICKEN AND PEPPER CASSEROLE

1 tablespoon ghee
½ green (bell) pepper, ½ red (bell) pepper and ½ yellow/orange (bell) pepper, all deseeded and sliced 3-cm/1¼-in. thick
2 onions, halved and sliced
8 chicken thighs, skin on and bone in
2 garlic cloves, crushed
1 tablespoon smoked paprika
1 teaspoon onion powder
1 teaspoon mustard powder
2 teaspoons salt
2 teaspoons coconut sugar
½ teaspoon dried marjoram or oregano
½ teaspoon dried thyme
1 tablespoon red wine vinegar
250 g/9 oz. passata/strained tomatoes

Serves 4

A great combination of flavours – Cajun spices with peppers and chicken. This is sure to be a crowd-pleaser.

Press the Sauté button on the multi-cooker and add the ghee. When hot, add half the (bell) peppers, all the onions and all the chicken thighs. Sauté until the onions are translucent. Remember to deglaze the pan (see page 4) with a splash of water to make sure the base of the pan has no bits stuck to the bottom.

Meanwhile, create a Cajun paste – mix the garlic, paprika, onion powder, mustard powder, salt, sugar, herbs and red wine vinegar in a small bowl. Add this to the pot and stir. Finally, add the passata/strained tomatoes and stir again.

Secure the lid in place and set to Poultry for 15 minutes. At the end of cooking, use the NPR method (see page 4). Stir in the remaining (bell) peppers and leave to mellow for a couple of minutes before serving. Great served over Cauliflower Rice (see page 85).

BEEF AND PAPRIKA STEW

1 tablespoon ghee or butter
1 onion, chopped
450 g/1 lb. casserole/stewing beef, roughly chopped
1 courgette/zucchini, chopped into 3-cm/1¼-in. lengths
3 sweet potatoes, peeled and chopped into 3 x 3-cm/1¼ x 1¼-in. pieces
2 large carrots, chopped into 3-cm/1¼-in. lengths
2 teaspoons sea salt
1 teaspoon mixed herbs
1½ teaspoons smoked paprika, plus extra to serve
1 teaspoon garlic powder
1 teaspoon onion powder
2 tablespoons tomato paste or beetroot/beet ketchup
1½ teaspoons Worcestershire sauce (gluten-free if preferred)
soured/sour cream, to serve

Serves 4

Inspired by a recipe given to me by a Hungarian friend, this stew is full of flavour and the meat is simply melt-in-the-mouth gorgeous.

Press the Sauté button on the multi-cooker and add the ghee or butter. When melted, add the onion and stewing beef. Sauté until the beef is no longer pink, then add the courgette/zucchini, sweet potatoes and carrots. Stir to combine, then add all the seasonings and stir once more.

Secure the lid in place and set to Stew for 30 minutes. Make sure the steam valve is closed. At the end of cooking, use the NPR method (see page 4). Serve with a generous dollop of soured/sour cream on top and a sprinkling of smoked paprika.

MUM'S BEEF STEW

1 teaspoon olive oil
1 large onion, chopped
2 garlic cloves, sliced
2 celery stalks, thickly sliced
4 carrots, thickly sliced
3 potatoes, unpeeled, chopped to same size pieces as the carrots
800 g/1 lb. 12 oz. casserole/stewing beef, cubed
200 ml/¾ cup red wine
1 tablespoon date nectar or honey
1 tablespoon tomato paste
1 teaspoon dried mixed herbs
1 teaspoon salt
1 teaspoon smoked paprika

Serves 4

This is a firm favourite in our family. The combination of smoky paprika and sweet honey combines with the beef and veggies to create a really hearty stew.

Press the Sauté button on the multi-cooker and add the oil. When hot, add all the vegetables and the beef. Stir for about 7 minutes. Don't worry if not all the beef is coloured.

Meanwhile, mix together the red wine, date nectar or honey, tomato paste and herbs. Add the salt and paprika to the pot and stir, then add the red wine mix and deglaze the pan (see page 4).

Secure the lid in place and set to Stew for 35 minutes. At the end of cooking, use the NPR method (see page 4) for 20 minutes, then use the QPR method and serve.

CAJUN PULLED CHICKEN

2 tablespoons vegetable stock paste (see page 31)
500 g/1 lb. 2 oz. boneless chicken breasts, sliced into 100-g/3½-oz. pieces
½ teaspoon Cajun spice mix

HONEY AND MUSTARD DRESSING
110 g/½ cup mayonnaise
60 ml/4 tablespoons extra virgin olive oil
2 tablespoons red wine vinegar
2 tablespoons raw honey
2 tablespoons Dijon mustard
1 tablespoon chopped onion
½ teaspoon sea salt

Serves 4

A combination of flavours and textures that is sure to please. This succulent and beautifully spiced pulled chicken is ideal served with a mixed salad.

To make the dressing, place all the ingredients in a blender and blend thoroughly. Set aside.

Mix the stock paste with 100 ml/⅓ cup water in the multi-cooker. Add the chicken pieces and sprinkle over the Cajun spice.

Secure the lid in place and set to Poultry for 10 minutes. At the end of cooking, use the NPR method (see page 4). Open the lid once the pressure has released. Shred the chicken using a couple of forks or a blunt knife and a fork – it should break away easily. Serve with a mixed salad and a drizzle of the honey and mustard dressing.

SMOKY BARBECUE CHICKEN

2–3 chicken breasts
6–7 carrots, cut into 3-cm/1¼-in. lengths

MARINADE
50 g/2 oz. passata/strained tomatoes
2½ teaspoons tomato purée
3 tablespoons molasses or black treacle
1 tablespoon maple syrup
¾ tablespoon apple cider vinegar
2 teaspoons salt
1½ teaspoons smoked paprika (or slightly less if you don't like too much heat)
1 teaspoon wholegrain mustard
½ teaspoon garlic powder

Serves 2–3

The appealing flavour of this dish comes from the addition of molasses or black treacle and paprika.

In a large container, mix together the marinade ingredients, then place the chicken breasts in the marinade. Place in the fridge and leave to marinate for at least 30 minutes, but ideally for a couple of hours.

When you are ready to cook, place everything into the multi-cooker. Secure the lid in place and set to Manual or High Pressure for 10 minutes. At the end of cooking, leave for 5 minutes, then use the QPR method (see page 4), then serve.

WHOLE ROAST LEMON CHICKEN

1 teaspoon smoked paprika
1 teaspoon dried thyme
½ teaspoon garlic salt
¾ teaspoon salt
¼ teaspoon ground black pepper
1 x 1.8-kg/4-lb. chicken
½ lemon
1 tablespoon ghee or coconut oil
300 ml/1¼ cups chicken stock (if using a stock cube, omit the salt from the seasoning)
3 tablespoons red wine
3 large potatoes, peeled and cut into quarters

Serves 4

This is such an impressive way to serve up an evening meal. Roast chicken no longer has to be reserved for Sundays when you can make one this simply and quickly in the pot.

In a small bowl or ramekin, mix together the smoked paprika, dried thyme, garlic powder, salt, and pepper. Rub the dry seasoning over the skin of the chicken. Put the lemon half inside the chicken cavity.

Press the Sauté button on the multi-cooker and add the ghee or coconut oil. When hot, push the chicken down into the pot. Try to sear all surfaces of the chicken by moving it around and pushing it down onto the base of the pot. Once seared on all surfaces, take the chicken out carefully and rest on a plate.

Add the stock and red wine to the pot, ensuring you deglaze the pot with a wooden spoon (see page 4). Add the potatoes to the pot and rest the trivet on top, being careful not to burn yourself on the hot inner pot. Place the chicken on the trivet.

Secure the lid in place and set to Manual or High Pressure for 30 minutes. At the end of cooking, use the NPR method (see page 4).

To serve, place the chicken and potatoes on a serving plate, and serve the sauce separately in a small jug/pitcher.

LEG OF LAMB IN RED WINE JUS

1 tablespoon butter
1.5–2-kg/3¼–4½-lb. leg of lamb, bone in
2 onions, chopped
250 ml/1 cup red wine
1 tablespoon vegetable stock paste (see page 31) or 1 vegetable stock cube
4 large potatoes, peeled and chopped into thirds
10 carrots, left whole

Serves 6–8

In the early days of our marriage, my husband and I would rely on a particular 7-hour lamb recipe whenever we had guests. We knew it was a reliable and impressive recipe, so we just made sure we never served it to the same guests twice. We then tweaked it a little when the kids came along, to suit our collective tastes. So when I saw that Mike Vrobel from dadcooksdinner.com had recreated the original version in the multi-cooker, I cooked our version in the pot using his recommended cooking times. It works like a dream!

Press the Sauté button on the multi-cooker and add the butter. When melted, add the lamb and sear on all sides. This will take about 5 minutes. Remove the lamb to a plate.

Add the onions to the pot. If they start to stick a little, use some of the red wine to deglaze the pan (see page 4). Add the rest of the red wine and when it starts to evaporate, add 250 ml/1 cup water, the stock paste or cube, potatoes and carrots. Place the lamb joint on top.

Secure the lid in place and set to Manual or High Pressure for 90 minutes. At the end of cooking, use the NPR method (see page 4). Serve the lamb with the vegetables and some of the jus.

PORK BELLY WITH WHITE CABBAGE

35 ml/2 tablespoons tamari or coconut aminos
1 tablespoon honey
1 teaspoon freshly grated ginger
1/8 teaspoon ground allspice
2 garlic cloves, crushed
5 drops of brown rice vinegar
600 g/1 lb. 5 oz. pork belly, thickly sliced
1/2 white cabbage, sliced into thick wedges

Serves 4

A very easy dish that is cost-effective and a real palate pleaser.

In a medium bowl, combine the tamari or coconut aminos, honey, ginger, allspice, garlic and vinegar with 3 1/2 tablespoons water.

Press the Sauté button on the multi-cooker. When up to heat, add the pork belly and immediately pour over the tamari/coconut aminos mix. Deglaze the pot (see page 4) with a spoon as you move the pork slices around the pot. Once the pork slices are seared on all sides, add the cabbage wedges.

Secure the lid in place and set to Manual or High Pressure for 30 minutes. At the end of cooking, use the NPR method (see page 4). Serve with jacket sweet potatoes (see page 126).

WHOLE GAMMON

200 ml/3/4 cup (hard) cider
3 very large potatoes, peeled and cut into thirds lengthways (omit if making ham only)
4 whole carrots, trimmed (omit if making ham only)
1 teaspoon salt (omit if making ham only)
1 x unsmoked gammon joint

Serves 4–6

This is a great way to cook gammon as a family meal or to make ham for multiple family meals throughout the week. This method is actually the one chosen by a wonderful friend and Instant Pot® expert Maria Bravo. She recommends cooking your gammon for 11 minutes per 1 lb. (that's just under 450 g) and that's what works for me. So whatever your size of gammon you can use this method and simply adjust the time.

Place the cider and 100 ml/1/3 cup water in the multi-cooker. Add the vegetables to the pot, then the salt. Place the gammon joint on top of the vegetables.

Secure the lid in place and set to Manual or High Pressure for 11 minutes per 500 g/1 lb. 2 oz. of gammon. At the end of cooking, use the NPR method (see page 4). Serve the gammon sliced with the vegetables and some of the cooking liquid from the base of the pot.

COTTAGE PIE

1 tablespoon ghee or butter
1 onion, chopped
500 g/1 lb. 2 oz. minced/ground beef
2 carrots, chopped
1 celery stalk, chopped
1 tablespoon tomato ketchup (ideally a low-sugar version)
1 tablespoon tamari or coconut aminos
1 tablespoon barbecue sauce (ideally a low-sugar version)
1 tablespoon vegetable stock paste (see page 31) or 1 vegetable stock cube
300-g/10½-oz. canned chopped tomatoes
4 medium potatoes, peeled and cut into quarters
2 tablespoons butter
1 tablespoon almond milk
1 tablespoon arrowroot
2 tablespoons grated/shredded mature Cheddar, pecorino or vegan cheese

Serves 4

This is a lovely 'pot in pot' pie. That means the potatoes can cook at the same time as the sauce, but without being in the sauce.

Press the Sauté button on the multi-cooker and add the ghee or butter. When melted, add the onion and sauté for 5 minutes, then add the beef and stir until browned, breaking it up as you go. Add the carrots, celery, ketchup, tamari or coconut aminos, barbecue sauce, stock paste or cube and tomatoes, plus 100 ml/⅓ cup water and stir.

Line the steamer basket with foil and place the potatoes and 190 ml/¾ cup water in the steamer basket. Place the trivet (ideally a long-legged one) in the pot and place the steamer basket on top.

Secure the lid and set to Meat for 15 minutes. At the end of cooking, use the NPR method (see page 4).

Drain the potatoes, transfer to a bowl and mash them with the butter and almond milk until smooth. Cover the bowl with foil to keep the mashed potato warm.

Using a slotted spoon, spoon or transfer the meat mixture into the base of an oven dish. Cover with foil to keep warm. Take 4 tablespoons of the liquid in the pot and stir with the arrowroot. Add this back into the pot and press the Sauté button – the sauce will thicken after 5–6 minutes. Add this sauce to the meat, then spoon the mashed potato on top and sprinkle over the cheese. Pop under a preheated grill/broiler until the cheese is melted.

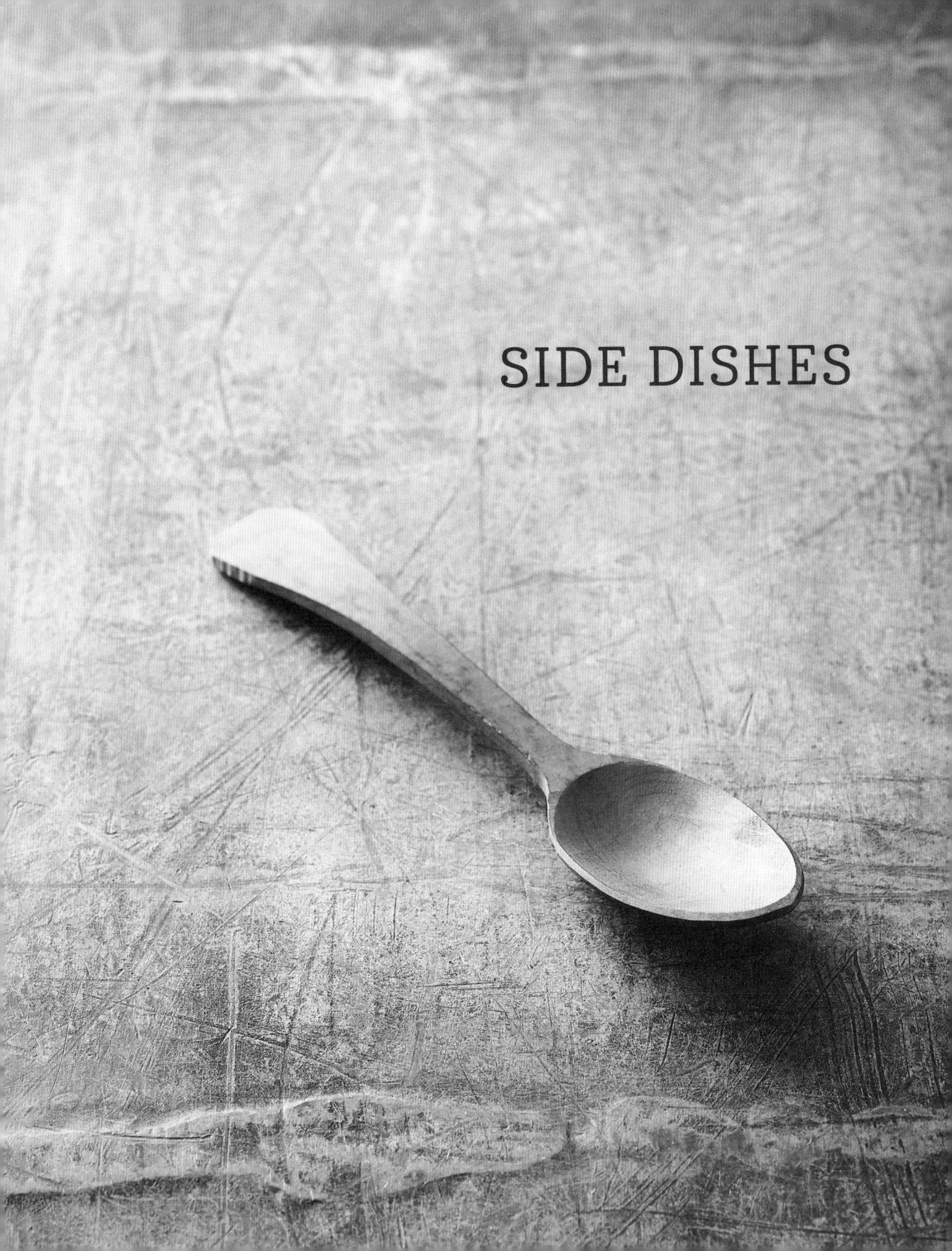

SIDE DISHES

BRUSSELS SPROUTS WITH BACON AND CHESTNUTS

1 tablespoon butter
4 slices of streaky bacon, chopped
20 Brussels sprouts, trimmed and scored on the bottom
1 tablespoon tamari or coconut aminos
120 g/4¼ oz. whole cooked chestnuts, peeled (you can buy these ready roasted in the supermarket)

Serves 4 as a side dish

I always jazz up Brussels sprouts – I think this stems from the early days of parenthood when I wasn't convinced the children would eat them without bells and whistles!

Press the Sauté button on the multi-cooker and add the butter. When melted, sauté the bacon until cooked, then add the Brussels sprouts, tamari or coconut aminos and 2 tablespoons water.

Secure the lid in place and set to Manual or High Pressure for 3 minutes. At the end of cooking, use the QPR method (see page 4). Add the chestnuts to the pan and stir until warmed through.

CAULIFLOWER MASH

1 cauliflower (about 500 g/ 1 lb. 2 oz. once leaves and most of stem removed)
1 teaspoon salt
1 teaspoon ground cumin
½ teaspoon coconut sugar
40 g/3 tablespoons salted butter or vegan spread

Serves 4 as a side dish

This dish provides the comfort of mashed potato but is much lower in carbohydrates and more nutritious. You may wonder why the cauliflower is cooked whole in this recipe. One reason is that it saves a lot of time, the other is that it avoids making a mess while chopping up the cauliflower at the start of cooking. Pressure cooking a whole cauliflower is so quick that you don't need to chop it up first to create deliciously creamy mash.

Carefully remove most of the cauliflower stem, but leave enough in place so that the florets stay intact. Place the cauliflower on the trivet in the multi-cooker. Add 250 ml/1 cup water to the pot. Sprinkle over the salt, cumin and coconut sugar.

Secure the lid in place and set to Manual or High Pressure for 10 minutes. At the end of cooking use the QPR method (see page 4).

Remove the cauliflower from the pot and place in a food processor (you may need to break it up a little to fit it in) with the butter or vegan spread. Process to a 'mashed potato' consistency, then serve.

BBQ BAKED BEANS

250 g/9 oz. dried haricot/navy beans, soaked overnight in a bowl with water to cover (yields 500 g/1 lb. 2 oz. once soaked)
1½ teaspoons salt
1 tablespoon molasses
1½ teaspoons maple syrup
½ teaspoon ground allspice
¼ teaspoon garlic powder
¼ teaspoon onion powder
50 g/3 tablespoons tomato purée/paste
300 g/10½ oz. passata/strained tomatoes
grated/shredded vegan or Cheddar cheese, to serve (optional)

Serves 4

Baked beans have become a British institution, yet they originated with Native Americans. This recipe is more authentic and closer to the original recipes than modern canned beans. While Native Americans used animal fat in their recipe, I've made this a vegan version.

Drain and rinse the soaked beans, then place them in the multi-cooker with all the other ingredients (except the cheese) and 150 ml/⅔ cup water.

Secure the lid in place and set to Manual or High Pressure for 25 minutes. At the end of cooking, use the NPR method (see page 4). Serve on slices of buttered sourdough toast or Grain-free Bread (see page 19). If you wish, scatter some grated cheese over the top.

JERK BAKED BEANS

1 tablespoon olive oil
1 onion, chopped
3 slices of streaky bacon, chopped into small pieces
2 x 400-g/14-oz. cans white beans (cannellini or haricot/navy beans work well), drained and rinsed
500 g/1 lb. 2 oz. passata/strained tomatoes
1 tablespoon honey
½ teaspoon treacle
½ teaspoon jerk seasoning
¼ teaspoon smoked paprika
⅛ teaspoon ground allspice
¾ teaspoon salt

Serves 8

This slightly spicy version of the classic baked beans makes a really delicious change.

Press the Sauté button on the multi-cooker and add the oil. When hot, add the onion and bacon and stir for about 5 minutes. Add all the other ingredients and stir to deglaze the pan (see page 4).

Secure the lid in place and set to Manual or High Pressure for 2 minutes. At the end of cooking, use the NPR method (see page 4). These beans taste delicious served on buttered sourdough toast or Grain-free Bread (see page 19).

RED CABBAGE

600 g/1 lb. 5 oz. red cabbage, shredded using a mandolin or sharp knife
2 eating apples, cored and grated
2 onions, chopped
1/4 teaspoon freshly grated nutmeg
1/4 teaspoon ground cloves
1/4 teaspoon ground cinnamon
1 tablespoon coconut sugar
1 teaspoon vegetable stock paste (see page 31) or 1/3 vegetable stock cube
3 tablespoons red wine vinegar
2 tablespoons butter or coconut oil
freshly ground black pepper

Serves 4–6 as a side dish

Spicy and sweet red cabbage complements many of the heartier dishes in this book.

Put the cabbage, apples and onions in the multi-cooker and sprinkle/drizzle over the spices, sugar, stock paste or cube and vinegar, plus 100 ml/1/3 cup water, then dot with the butter or coconut oil.

Secure the lid in place and set to Manual or High Pressure for 3 minutes. At the end of cooking, use the QPR method (see page 4), then serve.

GREEN CABBAGE, BACON AND LEEKS

25 g/1 3/4 tablespoons butter
4 slices of streaky bacon, chopped into small pieces
250 g/9 oz. thinly sliced leeks and sliced green cabbage, mixed together

Serves 4 as a side dish

This is a very quick and simple side dish. It is a great way to use up that last leek and the half a cabbage left over from Sunday lunch.

Press the Sauté button on the multi-cooker and add the butter. When melted, add the bacon and sauté until coloured. Add the vegetables and 1 tablespoon water and deglaze the pot (see page 4).

Secure the lid in place and set to Manual or High Pressure for 3 minutes. At the end of cooking, use the QPR method (see page 4), then serve.

CORN ON THE COB

3 corn on the cob/ears of corn, broken in half if you wish
3 tablespoons butter
freshly ground black pepper

Serves 3–6

This is simply the sweetest, quickest, tastiest way to prepare corn on the cob.

Pour 300 ml/1¼ cups water into the multi-cooker. Place the corn in the steaming basket on the trivet inside the pot.

Secure the lid in place and set to Manual or High Pressure for 3 minutes. At the end of cooking, use the QPR method (see page 4). Eat straight away, dotted with butter and black pepper.

'BAKED' JACKET SWEET POTATOES

3 x 230-g/8-oz. sweet potatoes, skins scrubbed in water using a potato brush or scouring cloth
3 teaspoons butter or soured/sour cream

Serves 3

No peeling. No fuss. No mess. This way of preparing sweet potatoes is hassle-free. The results are deliciously soft 'baked' sweet potatoes. These are tasty served with butter or soured/sour cream.

Place 250 ml/1 cup water in the base of the multi-cooker. Insert the metal trivet and place the potatoes on their sides on the trivet in a single layer.

Secure the lid in place and set to Manual or High Pressure for 20 minutes. At the end of cooking, use the QPR method (see page 4). Serve with a teaspoon of butter or soured/sour cream on each potato.

SWEET THINGS

'BAKED' APPLES WITH NUTTY FILLING

3 Bramley apples
60 g/4 tablespoons salted butter, at room temperature
60 g/4 tablespoons maple syrup
80 g/3/4 cup mixed chopped nuts (or chopped nuts of your choice)
1/2 teaspoon ground cinnamon
1/4 teaspoon ground ginger
1/4 teaspoon ground allspice

Serves 3

Cooking apples in the multi-cooker is a really quick way to create a tasty dessert. They're moist and full of flavour.

Remove the core from the apples. In a bowl, mix together the butter, maple syrup, nuts and spices. Cut three large squares of foil and place an apple upright on each. Fill the cored hole with the nut mixture. Wrap the apples in the foil.

Place 250 ml/1 cup water in the multi-cooker. Place the trivet in the pot and the foil-wrapped apples on top of the trivet.

Secure the lid in place and set to Manual or High Pressure for 10–15 minutes, depending on the size of the apples (very large apples will need the full 15 minutes). At the end of cooking, use the QPR method (see page 4), then serve.

SEEDED APPLE CRUMBLE

3 eating apples, peeled and cored
100 g/1 cup gluten-free rolled/ old-fashioned oats
50 g/1/3 cup mixed seeds
25 g/2 tablespoons coconut sugar
1/2 teaspoon ground cinnamon
75 g/1/3 cup salted butter
Greek yogurt, to serve

Serves 6

A deliciously comforting dish using the natural sweetness of apples to create a tasty base, and with seeds mixed with the crumble to give texture and a great flavour to the topping.

Chop the apples into wedges. Lay these in the base of a flat-bottomed, round heatproof glass dish.

In a separate bowl, mix together the oats, seeds, sugar and cinnamon, then add the butter and rub together with your fingertips. Spoon the crumble over the top of the layered apple.

Pour 300 ml/1 1/4 cups water into the multi-cooker. Add the trivet and place the crumble dish on top.

Secure the lid in place and set to Manual or High Pressure for 10 minutes. At the end of cooking, use the NPR method (see page 4). Serve warm or cold with Greek yogurt.

BUTTERNUT AND CINNAMON CHEESECAKE

BASE

160 g/5½ oz. gluten-free oatcakes
20 g/1½ tablespoons coconut sugar
80 g/5½ tablespoons butter, melted

TOPPING

2 tablespoons coconut flour
1 teaspoon ground cinnamon, plus extra for dusting
a pinch of salt
150 g/5½ oz. puréed steamed butternut squash
250 g/1¼ cups cream cheese
60 g/5 tablespoons coconut sugar
3 eggs

15-cm/6-in. diameter deep, round springform cake pan

Serves 8

This recipe is inspired by Julia Levy-Twomey who posted a version of this cheesecake on a social media group. Her opening gambit was 'I'm Jewish and I have New York in my veins...' before outlining how to pressure-cook the perfect cheesecake. That's the sort of commendation that sparks intrigue on my part and all I can say is that I am so glad she posted the original version, because this cheesecake is dreamy. My version is gluten-free, too.

Line the base of the cake pan with baking parchment.

For the base, in a food processor, grind the oatcakes and sugar to a powder, then add the melted butter and process again. Push this into the base of the cake pan, using the back of a cold spoon to achieve an even spread.

Put all the topping ingredients into your food processor and combine. Pour into the cake pan over the base. Wrap one sheet of foil over the pan, covering the top fully so the folds of foil are under the pan. Place the trivet in the multi-cooker and pour water into the pot up to trivet level. Place the cake pan on the trivet.

Secure the lid in place and set to Manual or High Pressure for 50 minutes. At the end of cooking, use the NPR method (see page 4). Leave to cool, then pop in the fridge for an hour before serving. Dust with cinnamon just before serving.

BANANA RICE PUDDING

1 tablespoon butter
500 ml/2 cups almond or coconut milk
110 g/scant 2/3 cup pudding rice (you can use Arborio rice, too)
2 tablespoons maple syrup, plus extra to serve if you wish
1/8 teaspoon ground nutmeg
1/4 teaspoon ground cinnamon
2 ripe bananas, peeled and sliced on the diagonal

Serves 4

This is a deliciously 'creamy' dessert made without dairy. The banana and cinnamon combine really well.

Press the Sauté button on the multi-cooker and add the butter. When melted, add the milk and bring to the boil. Stir in the rice.

Secure the lid in place and set to Rice for 12 minutes. At the end of cooking, use the QPR method (see page 4), but keep warm with the lid on for a further 15 minutes. Stir in the maple syrup, nutmeg, cinnamon and banana and leave for another 2 minutes, then serve.

CHOCOLATE PLANTAINS

50 g/3 1/2 tablespoons butter or coconut oil
25 g/1 2/3 tablespoons coconut sugar
a pinch of salt
1 tablespoon raw cacao powder
2 whole, ripe plantains, peeled and sliced 2-cm/3/4-in. thick
1 tablespoon nut butter (ideally almond or cashew), to serve

Serves 4

Plantain, a relative of the banana, make fantastic desserts. This recipe is inspired by a classic flavour combination. Cooking the plantains this way really does show them off at their best.

Press the Sauté button on the multi-cooker. Add the butter or coconut oil, coconut sugar, salt and cacao powder, plus 25 ml/scant 2 tablespoons water to the pot. Heat for a couple of minutes, then stir in the plantain slices to coat in the sauce.

Secure the lid in place and set to Manual or High Pressure for 3 minutes. At the end of cooking, use the QPR method (see page 4). Serve with a good dollop of almond or cashew butter over the top.

POACHED PEARS IN GRAPE JUICE

150 ml/⅔ cup red grape juice
40 g/3¼ tablespoons coconut sugar
1 cinnamon stick
2 cloves
2 ripe but firm pears, peeled, with their bottoms sliced off so they will sit upright
Greek or coconut yogurt, to serve

Serves 2

I don't know about you, but I am sometimes put off making poached pears in wine partly because I don't want to waste wine on pears and partly because of the quantities of sugar added to the wine. So this is a dish created to harness the nutritional value of grapes but with less sugar and no wasted wine.

Press the Sauté button on the multi-cooker and add the grape juice, sugar and spices. Heat until the sugar has melted and the sauce has reduced a little. Add the peeled pears to the pot.

Secure the lid in place and set to Manual or High Pressure for 7–8 minutes, depending on the size of the pears. At the end of cooking, use the QPR method (see page 4).

Serve with Greek or coconut yogurt.

CARROT CAKE

CAKE

95 g/scant 1/2 cup coconut sugar
140 g/10 tablespoons butter, softened
200 g/1 1/2 cups grated carrot
1 teaspoon ground cinnamon
2 eggs
2 1/2 teaspoons baking powder
135 g/1 cup wholemeal/whole-wheat spelt flour

FROSTING (OPTIONAL)

200 g/scant 1 1/2 cups icing/confectioner's sugar
50 g/3 tbsp butter, at room temperature
200 g/scant 1 cup cream cheese

15-cm/6-in. diameter round non-stick springform cake pan

Serves 8

Who doesn't love a carrot cake? This recipe produces a moist and sweet cake that is hard to resist.

Mix all the cake ingredients together in a bowl. Pour the batter into the cake pan and place on the trivet. Add 450 ml/scant 2 cups water to the multi-cooker and lower the trivet and pan into the inner pot.

Secure the lid in place and set to Manual or High Pressure for 30 minutes. At the end of cooking, use the NPR method (see page 4) for 15 minutes, then use the QPR method. Be careful when you remove the lid not to drip any liquid onto the cake – if necessary, use a paper towel to dab excess water off the cake.

For the frosting, beat the icing/confectioner's sugar and butter together in a stand mixer (or use a handheld electric whisk). Add the cream cheese and beat until fully combined. Once the cake is cool, spread the frosting in a thick layer over the top.

BANANA OAT SPONGE CAKES

a little oil, such as coconut oil, or melted butter, for greasing
2 bananas, peeled
2 eggs
120 g/1 1/4 cups gluten-free rolled/old-fashioned oats
100 ml/1/3 cup almond milk
1/4 teaspoon baking powder
1/2 teaspoon ground cinnamon
40 g/2 3/4 tablespoons date nectar or maple syrup
cream or Greek yogurt, to serve

4 ramekins

Makes 4

Oats are rich in fibre and are actually higher in protein than many other grains. These little cakes are a really tasty and substantial dessert. They are best eaten soon after cooking.

Using a pastry brush, brush the insides of the ramekins evenly with the oil or melted butter. In a food processor, mix all the ingredients except the cream or yogurt together to form a thick batter. Pour an equal amount of the batter into each ramekin. Put 500 ml/2 cups water into the multi-cooker. Put the trivet in the pot and place the ramekins on top (two in the 6-litre pot or four in the 8-litre pot).

Secure the lid in place and set to Manual or High Pressure for 1 minute. At the end of cooking, use the NPR method (see page 4) for 5 minutes, then the QPR method. Remove the ramekins and run a knife around the edge of each to release the cakes, or serve them in the ramekins. These are best eaten warm, straight from the pot, with cream or Greek yogurt.

ALMOND CHOCOLATE BROWNIE CAKE

100 g/scant ¾ cup plain/ bittersweet chocolate, broken into squares
100 g/7 tablespoons butter
70 g/5⅔ tablespoons coconut sugar
100 g/1 cup ground almonds
3 eggs
fresh raspberries, to serve

15-cm/6-in. round non-stick springform cake pan

Serves 6

This is a deliciously moist chocolate brownie cake made without any grain-based flours.

Melt the chocolate and butter in a medium saucepan over a gentle heat. Once melted, add the sugar and stir to combine. Stir in the ground almonds and then leave to cool.

In a separate bowl, beat the eggs until fluffy. Gently fold the eggs into the cooled chocolate mixture and pour into the cake pan. Pour 250 ml/ 1 cup water into the multi-cooker. Put the trivet into the pot, then place the cake pan on top.

Secure the lid in place and set to Manual or High Pressure for 12 minutes. At the end of cooking, use the QPR method (see page 4). Remove the cake pan and trivet from the pot and leave the cake to cool a little. If necessary, remove any drips of water on the surface of the cake with paper towels.

Serve at room temperature with fresh raspberries on the side.

GLOSSARY

Barbecue Sauce – try to find one without added sugar.

Coconut Aminos – this is a soy-free alternative to soy sauce or tamari. Some coconut aminos taste very sweet. The ideal one is a salty-tasting sauce that can be used in place of soy sauce or tamari for those who want to avoid soy products.

Coconut Sugar – while coconut sugar is still a sugar and therefore to be used sparingly, it raises blood sugar more slowly than white granulated sugar so is a preferred option. It's produced from the nectar of coconut flower buds. The buds are cut open and the sap is captured, and then boiled down.

Fish Sauce – there are many brands on the market. I recommend using one without added sugar.

Stevia – this sugar alternative comes in powder form and is derived from the stevia leaf. It is reported to have no effect on blood sugar levels. You need to use such small amounts of this powder to sweeten foods that it is a useful and cost-effective natural sweetener to use in dessert recipes.

Stock Paste – there are many recipes in this book that call for stock cubes or stock paste. You are welcome to use either. I prefer stock paste because that way I know what's gone into the stock. There's a recipe for vegetable stock paste on page 31.

Tamari – this is gluten-free soy sauce.

Tomato Ketchup – try to find a reduced sugar or no added sugar version.

INDEX

A

almonds: almond chocolate brownie cake 140
almond satay 77
apples: apple puree 12
'baked' apples with nutty filling 131
seeded apple crumble 131
apricot turkey meatballs 58
aubergines (eggplants):
aubergine and cauliflower vegan curry 90
aubergine and white sweet potato bhaji curry 93

B

bacon: Brussels sprouts with bacon and chestnuts 121
cauliflower and bacon soup 24
chicken and bacon risotto 64
chickpea, potato and bacon soup 28
green cabbage, bacon and leeks 125
split pea and bacon soup 36
vegetable and bacon soup 36
bananas: banana oat sponge cakes 139
banana rice pudding 135
spelt banana bread 16
beans: BBQ baked beans 122
jerk baked beans 122
beef: beef and paprika stew 107
beef Bolognese 50
beef massaman 78
cheese-filled meatballs in a chunky tomato sauce 57
chilli beef and mushrooms 94
cottage pie 116
meatballs with lentil pasta 58
mild chilli beef with sweet potato and black beans 93
Mum's beef stew 107
red Thai beef curry 78
Bircher muesli, grain-free 11
biriyani, speedy vegetable 68
black beans, mild chilli beef with 93
Bolognese sauce 50
bone broth 32
bread, grain-free 19
Brussels sprouts with bacon and chestnuts 121
butternut squash:
butternut and chorizo golden rice 67
butternut and cinnamon cheesecake 132
butternut squash, chorizo and onion on courgetti 54
butternut squash, spinach and chickpea soup 27
mild butternut dhal 86

C

cabbage: green cabbage, bacon and leeks 125
pork belly with white cabbage 115
red cabbage 125
cacciatore, chicken 104
Cajun chicken and pepper casserole 104
Cajun pulled chicken 108
cakes: almond chocolate brownie cake 140
banana oat sponge cakes 139
carrot cake 139
spelt banana bread 16
carrots: carrot and cashew hummus 41
carrot and ginger soup 23
carrot cake 139
cashew nuts: carrot and cashew hummus 41
cashew nut pilaff 63
casseroles: Cajun chicken and pepper casserole 104
see also stews; tagines
cauliflower: aubergine and cauliflower vegan curry

90
cauliflower and bacon soup 24
cauliflower mash 121
cauliflower, white sweet potato and chorizo soup 24
green bean and cauliflower curry 90
Thai chicken with cauliflower rice 85
chana masala quinoa 86
cheese: aromatic paneer curry 81
cheese-filled meatballs in a chunky tomato sauce 57
courgette, feta and mint risotto 63
cheesecake, butternut and cinnamon 132
chestnuts: Brussels sprouts with bacon and chestnuts 121
chestnut and vegetable soup 35
chicken: Cajun chicken and pepper casserole 104
Cajun pulled chicken 108
chicken and bacon risotto 64
chicken cacciatore 104
chicken tikka masala 77
Malaysian chicken 85
Mediterranean chicken with rice 71
smoky barbecue chicken 108
Thai chicken with cauliflower rice 85
whole roast lemon chicken 111
chicken liver pâté 41
chickpeas: butternut squash, spinach and chickpea soup 27
carrot and cashew hummus 41
chana masala quinoa 86
chickpea, potato and bacon soup 28
curried chickpea soup 23
Sam's soup 28
chillies: chilli beef and mushrooms 94
mild chilli beef with sweet potato and black beans 93
chocolate: almond chocolate brownie cake 140
chocolate plantains 135
chorizo: butternut squash and chorizo golden rice 67
butternut squash, chorizo and onion on courgetti 54
cauliflower, white sweet potato and chorizo soup 24
chowder, dairy-free fish 32
compote, rhubarb and raspberry 15
cottage pie 116
courgettes (zucchinis): butternut squash, chorizo and onion on courgetti 54
courgette, feta and mint risotto 63
sausage and tomato sauce with courgetti 54
crisp, raspberry 15
crumble, seeded apple 131
curry: aromatic paneer curry 81
aubergine and cauliflower vegan curry 90
aubergine and white sweet potato bhaji curry 93
beef massaman with new potatoes 78
chicken tikka masala 77
curried chickpea soup 23
green bean and cauliflower curry 90
red Thai beef curry 78
speedy vegetable biriyani 68
spinach and potato curry 82
vegetable curry 81

D E

dhal, mild butternut 86
dosa, Indian spinach with 82
eggs: spinach and salmon egg cups 45
sweet potato and pancetta frittata 42

F

fennel: smoked haddock with fennel and mushrooms 49
fish: cod in Parma ham 49
dairy-free fish chowder 32
salmon supper with sweet potatoes 45
smoked haddock with fennel and mushrooms 49
smoked salmon kedgeree 46
spinach and salmon egg cups 45
French onion soup 31
frittata, sweet potato and pancetta 42

G H

gammon, whole 115
grape juice, poached pears in 136
green bean and cauliflower curry 90
hummus, carrot and cashew 41

I J

Indian spinach with dosa 82
jerk baked beans 122

K L

kedgeree, smoked salmon 46
lamb: lamb rack stew 99
lamb sag 89
lamb tagine 100
leg of lamb in red wine jus 112
Moroccan lamb 100
leeks, green cabbage, bacon and 125
lentil pasta, meatballs with 58
lentils: mild butternut dhal 86

M

Malaysian chicken 85
meatballs: apricot turkey meatballs 58
cheese-filled meatballs in a chunky tomato sauce 57
meatballs with lentil pasta 58
Mediterranean chicken with rice 71
Moroccan lamb 100
muesli, grain-free Bircher 11
Mum's beef stew 107
mushrooms: chilli beef and mushrooms 94
mushroom quin-otto 72
mushroom risotto 64
smoked haddock with fennel and mushrooms 49

N O

nuts: 'baked' apples with nutty filling 131
oats: banana oat sponge cakes 139
simple dairy-free, gluten-free porridge 12
onion soup, French 31

P

pancetta: pancetta and tomato pasta 53
sweet potato and pancetta frittata 42
paneer: aromatic paneer curry 81
Parma ham, cod in 49
pasta: all-in-one spaghetti Bolognese 50
meatballs with lentil pasta 58
pancetta and tomato pasta 53
pea and paprika creamy pasta 53
pâté, chicken liver 41
pears: poached pears in grape juice 136
peas: pea and corn rice 68
pea and paprika creamy pasta 53
peppers: Cajun chicken and pepper casserole 104
pilaffs: cashew nut pilaff 63
quinoa pilaff 72
plantains, chocolate 135
pork: pork belly with white cabbage 115
Spanish rice with minced pork 67
spicy minced pork 94
whole gammon 115

porridge, simple dairy-free gluten-free 12
potatoes: beef massaman with new potatoes 78
chickpea, potato and bacon soup 28
cottage pie 116
spinach and potato curry 82

Q R

quinoa: chana masala quinoa 86
mushroom quin-otto 72
quinoa pilaff 72
raspberry crisp 15
raspberries: raspberry crisp 15
rhubarb and raspberry compote 15
rice: banana rice pudding 135
butternut squash and chorizo golden rice 67
cashew nut pilaff 63
chicken and bacon risotto 64
courgette, feta and mint risotto 63
Mediterranean chicken with rice 71
mushroom risotto 64
pea and corn rice 68
smoked salmon kedgeree 46
Spanish rice with minced pork 67
speedy vegetable biriyani 68

S

saag 82
sag aloo 82
Sam's soup 28
satay, almond 77
sausage and tomato sauce with courgetti 54
seafood stew 103
seeded apple crumble 131
soups 20–37
bone broth 32
butternut squash, spinach and chickpea soup 27
carrot and ginger soup 23
cauliflower and bacon soup 24
cauliflower, white sweet potato and chorizo soup 24
chestnut and vegetable soup 35
chickpea, potato and bacon soup 28
curried chickpea soup 23
dairy-free fish chowder 32
French onion soup 31
Sam's soup 28
split pea and bacon soup 36
vegetable and bacon soup 36
Spanish rice with minced pork 67
spelt banana bread 16
spinach: butternut squash, spinach and chickpea soup 27
Indian spinach with dosa 82
lamb sag 89
spinach and potato curry 82
spinach and salmon egg cups 45
split pea and bacon soup 36
stews: beef and paprika stew 107
lamb rack stew 99
Mum's beef stew 107
seafood stew 103
stock paste, vegetable 31
sweet potatoes: aubergine and white sweet potato bhaji curry 93
'baked' jacket sweet potatoes 126
cauliflower, white sweet potato and chorizo soup 24
mild chilli beef with sweet potato and black beans 93
salmon supper with sweet potatoes 45
sweet potato and pancetta frittata 42
sweetcorn: corn on the cob 126
pea and corn rice 68

T

tagines: lamb tagine 100
Moroccan lamb 100
Thai beef curry 78
Thai chicken with cauliflower rice 85
tikka masala, chicken 77
tomatoes: cheese-filled meatballs in a chunky tomato sauce 57
pancetta and tomato pasta 53
sausage and tomato sauce with courgetti 54
turkey meatballs, apricot 58

V

vegetables: chestnut and vegetable soup 35
cod in Parma ham with vegetables 49
speedy vegetable biriyani 68
vegetable and bacon soup 36
vegetable curry 81
vegetable stock paste 31

ACKNOWLEDGEMENTS

This book wouldn't have been possible without the help of my incredible literary agent who sees opportunity in unexpected places. Jane Graham-Maw was ready to support me in my endeavours to build on my previous book and provide more quick and simple real-food meal solutions for busy people.

Maria Bravo got me hooked on my Instant Pot® with her inspiring and encouraging social media posts. Subsequently, Maria has been very supportive of me while I worked to produce and test healthy recipes for the Instant Pot®.

To my recipe testers – Maria Bravo, Kate Hart, Alli Wiltshire, Pat Duckworth and June Bailey – thank you for your help and guidance, as well as testing and advising on recipe tweaks.

Finally, to my family who have enjoyed the experience of tasting lots of different meals each day, be that in the evenings or the next day in their lunchboxes. They are so incredibly supportive and have been great company during those long hours spent testing recipes in the kitchen.